MYTHMAKERS & LAWBREAKERS
anarchist writers on fiction

edited by
Margaret Killjoy

introduction by
Kim Stanley Robinson

AK
PRESS
EDINBURGH · OAKLAND · BALTIMORE

Mythmakers and Lawbreakers: Anarchist Writers on Fiction
Edited by Margaret Killjoy, 2009

ISBN-13: 978-1-849350-02-0

Library of Congress Control Number: 2009932861

This edition published by AK Press:

AK Press	AK Press UK
674-A 23rd Street	PO Box 12766
Oakland, CA 94612	Edinburgh EH8 9YE
USA	Scotland
WWW.AKPRESS.ORG	WWW.AKUK.COM
akpress@akpress.org	ak@akdin.demon.co.uk

The above addresses would be delighted to provide you with the latest AK Press distribution
catalog, which features several thousand books, pamphlets, zines, audio and video recordings,
and gear, all published or distributed by AK Press. Alternately, visit our website to browse the
catalog and find out the latest news from the world of anarchist publishing: WWW.AKPRESS.ORG &
REVOLUTIONBYTHEBOOK.AKPRESS.ORG.

Many of these interviews originally published by Strangers In A Tangled Wilderness:
WWW.TANGLEDWILDERNESS.ORG
Margaret Killjoy can be found online at: WWW.BIRDSBEFORETHESTORM.NET
Further material is available at: WWW.ANARCHISTFICTION.NET
Cover Art by Colin Foran: WWW.COLINFORAN.COM

Fonts we used:
tw cen MT
Warnoc Pro
HEADLINE HPLHS ONE
Black Gothic HPLHS Condensed Black
𝒮𝑒𝓁𝒻𝒾𝓈𝒽 (Selfish)

Printed in Canada on acid-free, recycled paper with union labor.

Contents

Introduction
KIM STANLEY ROBINSON

THIS BOOK COLLECTS FOURTEEN INTERVIEWS WITH WRITERS who have either described themselves as anarchists, written about anarchists in historical or contemporary settings, or invented fictional cultures that they or others have called anarchist. Each person's story is different, naturally, and the definitions they have given for anarchism are not the same either. An-archy: absence of rulers, or absence of law? The original Greek suggests the former, common English usage since the seventeenth century, the latter; and it makes quite a difference which definition you use. So we find those interviewed here circling repeatedly around questions of definition, both of what the concept means, and how it can be applied to writing and to life, not only the lives of those included here, but the lives of everyone. These are knotty problems, and it's no surprise that the questions and answers here keep pulling and prodding at them, hoping for some clarity.

Another problem the interviews return to again and again is how to reconcile anarchist beliefs with actual life in the globalized capitalist system. Some of the writers here live by anarchist beliefs to a certain extent, publishing or distributing their writing outside the conventional publishing world, or living in alternative arrangements of one kind or another. Others live more outwardly conventional lives, while writing about anarchism and supporting it in their political action, of which writing is one part. No one can escape a certain amount of contradiction here; the world economy is almost entirely capitalist in structure, and state rule is an overarching reality in human affairs. So the interest in anarchism expressed by these writers, and the effect this complex of ideas has on their lives, has necessarily to involve various compromises and what might be called symbolic actions—as long as one remembers that symbolic actions are also real actions, not at all to be dismissed. Voting is a symbolic action, going to church is a symbolic action, speaking and writing and talking are symbolic actions; all are also real actions, and have real effects in the real world—partly by themselves, and partly by what they suggest symbolically we should do in all the rest of our actions.

Here, therefore we are talking about ideology. I mean this in the way defined by Louis Althusser, which is roughly that an ideology is an imaginary relationship to a real situation. Both parts of the definition exist: there is a real situation, and by necessity our relationship to it is partly an imaginary one. So we all have an ideology, and in fact would be disabled or overwhelmed without one. The question then becomes, can we improve our ideology, in terms of both individual and collective function, and if so, how?

Here is where anarchist ideas come strongly into play. We live in a destructive and unjust system, which is nevertheless so massively entrenched, so protected by money, law, and armed force, as to seem unchangeable, even nature itself; it strives to seem natural, so much so that it would be very difficult to imagine a way out or a way forward from the current state. Given this reality of our moment in history, what should we do? What can we do, right now, that would change the situation?

One of the first and most obvious answers is: resist the current system in every way that is likely to do some good. That answer might rule out certain responses: people have been resisting capitalism for well over a century now, and many of the first methods to occur to people have been tried and have failed. Spontaneous mass revolt has been tried and has usually failed. Organized insurrection has sometimes done better, but over the long haul has often rebounded in ways that worsened the situation. Labor action and legal reform often seem possible and sometimes have achieved tangible success, but again, ultimately, despite what they have achieved, we find ourselves in the situation we are in now, so obviously labor action and legal reform are not as effective as one would hope. Mass political education has for a long time been a goal of those interested in promoting change, and again successes can be pointed to, but the overall impact has not yet been effective enough to avoid the danger we find ourselves in. What then should we do?

One thing that would help is to have some idea of what we might be trying to change toward; and this is where anarchism plays its part. As such it is a utopian political vision, and this is why several of the writers interviewed in this book are science fiction writers who have written stories describing anarchist situations as utopian spaces, as better systems that we should be struggling to achieve. This is my own situation; as a leftist, interested in opposing capitalism and to changing it to something more just and sustainable, I have once or twice tried to depict societies with anarchist aspects or roots. These, like the work of other science fiction writers, are thought experiments, designed to explore ideas by way of fictional scenarios. Problems can be discussed by way of dramatizations, and the appeal of an alternative society can be evoked for people to contemplate, to wish for, to work for. Until we have a vision of what we are working for, it is very hard to choose what to do in the present to get there.

Here is where anarchism has its greatest appeal, as well as its greatest danger. It is a rather pure and simple political system. It says that left to ourselves (or educated properly), people can be trusted to be good; that if we were not twisted by the demands of money and the state, we would take care of each other better than we do now. In a way, this is a view that merely extends democratic thinking to its end point: if we are all equal, if everyone together rules equally, then no one rules; and thus you expand democracy until it ends up at anarchy. It is a profoundly hopeful view, and hope for a different state is a crucial component of action. Here in particular, symbolic action is also at the same time real action.

One way of putting this, used more than once by the writers in this book, is that society is now organized vertically, in a hierarchy of power, privilege, prosperity, and health, which is structured in almost the same demographic pyramid as feudalism, or even the ancient warrior-priest command states. Anarchism suggests that the great majority of us would be far better off in a horizontal arrangement, an association of equals. Such a horizontality in the realm of power used to be derided as hopelessly naïve and unrealistic, but the more we learn about our human past and our primate ancestors, the more it becomes clear that this was the norm during the entirety of our evolution; only since the invention of agriculture, patriarchy, and the warrior-priest power structure has verticality ruled our lives. Getting back to a horizontal structure would be a return to the species norm and collective sanity, and to a sense of justice that long predates humanity itself, as can be seen clearly in the actions of our primate cousins.

From vertical to horizontal, then; but this is the work of democracy too, and even the work of history itself, if progress in human welfare is what we judge history by. So the more we succeed in this long work, the closer we come to the goals of anarchism, and the goals of other utopian endeavors: democracy, science, justice.

In the meantime, we have to constantly work; resist capitalism; interrogate our own actions; and speak out against the current order, for something better. That's what these writers have been doing in their lives and their work, and so this book too becomes part of that project. It's been going on for a very long time, and will presumably continue past our moment; but our destruction of the biosphere has moved the whole process into crisis mode, and we won't be leaving that mode until the crisis is resolved. So to a certain extent, we can no longer take the long view. We have to avert a biophysical catastrophe if we want to give our children a healthy planet and civilization. In this moment of the storm, all our political ideas need to be reconsidered, even the most radical ones, or especially the most radical ones. And all those based on a hopeful view of humanity, and those that help us to construct a utopian project for us to fulfill as soon as possible, deserve to be brought into the discussion. So: read on, and imagine a horizontal world, a free association of six billion equals. And, as Brecht said, "If you think this is utopian, please also consider why it is such."

Editor's Note

As Derrick Jensen said to me, "Any book that doesn't start from the fact that this culture is killing the planet and work to resolve it is unforgiveable." So why was I writing fiction?

I started this project that you hold in your hands in the spring of 2007. I had been writing a lot of short stories and had just published my first widely-read piece, "Yena of Angeline and the Tale of the Terrible Townies." I started wondering who else was doing what I was doing, which other anarchists were writing fiction. Moreover, I started wondering why. What could we hope to accomplish through storytelling? So I went on down to the San Francisco Anarchist Bookfair, which is the largest anarchist bookfair in the US, to scour up some fiction. I didn't find much; in fact, I only came back with two thin novels. I decided the whole thing needed a bit more active research. And like any good zinemaker, I decided I would collect everything I figured out into a zine of some sort.

The first thing I did was write Ursula K. Le Guin a letter, and it was the best possible first step. Her interest in the project spurred me forward, and it didn't hurt that so many of the other authors I interviewed are fans of her work. I spent two years tracking down anarchist authors from as wide of a spectrum as possible. Somewhere along the way it became book length, and AK Press agreed to publish it.

I don't think it's any stretch of the imagination to say that not all of the authors I talked to would agree with each other about much more than the desire for an anarchist society, if that. I've spoken with pacifists and insurrectionary anarchists, with anti-civilization authors and pro-technology ones. But they've all got a lot to say about storytelling, a lot to say about society. I'm glad to get them under one cover.

"An anarchist is one who, choosing, accepts the responsibility of choice."

—Ursula K. Le Guin

URSULA K. LE GUIN

Ursula K. Le Guin stands as one of the strongest voices in feminist science fiction. The author of the gender-bending The Left Hand of Darkness *and the anarchist novel* The Dispossessed, *she unabashedly explores the complexities of anti-authoritarian feminist society with a brilliantly poetic voice. Many of her other, less-explicitly anarchist fictions also delve into societies built on mutual aid, and the whole of her work comes highly recommended.*

I wrote her a letter and requested an interview. It was the first interview I conducted for the project, and to say I was nervous would be a bit of an understatement: I've read Ursula's essays and novels with a bright-eyed enthusiasm for many years. We spoke about the role of politics in writing, about her introduction to anarchism, and (because I'm a feminist grammar nerd) about the use of the singular "they" in English.

Margaret: *One of the things that I'm quite curious to explore is the role of the radical as an author of fiction. What do you feel like you've accomplished, on a social/political level, with your writing? Do you have any specific examples of change that you've helped initiate?*

Ursula: I may agree with Shelley that poets are the unacknowledged legislators of the world, but he didn't mean they really get many laws enacted, and I guess I didn't ever really look for definable, practical results of anything I wrote. My utopias are not blueprints. In fact, I distrust utopias that pretend to be blueprints. Fiction is not a good medium for preaching or for planning. It is really good, though, for what we used to call consciousness-raising.

Within my field of work—imaginative fiction—I think I have had an appreciable effect on the representation of gender and of "race," specifically skin color. When I came into the field, the POV was totally male-centric and everybody was white. At first I wrote that way too. In science fiction, I joined the feminist movement when it reawoke in the late sixties, early seventies, and we did away with the squeaking Barbies and began to write actual women characters. In fantasy, my heroes were colored people when, as far as I know, nobody else's were. (And yet I still fight, every single fantasy jacket-cover, to get them represented as nonwhite).

Margaret: *From the other direction, do you ever feel pressured from the "radical" crowd to be writing "more politically" or along certain lines?*

Ursula: I don't put myself in a position to get much pressure from anybody. I am not a joiner, and I lay low in public (except for stuff like protest marches, which I have been doing for the last millennium.)

Of course, I have been scolded by Marxists for not being Marxist, but they scold everybody for not being Marxist. And activist anarchists always hope I might be an activist, but I think they realize that I would be a lousy one, and let me go back to writing what I write.

Jefferson thought we already had liberty as an inalienable right, and only had to pursue happiness. I think the pursuit of liberty is what the Left is mostly about. But also, I think if you really want to pursue liberty, as an artist, you cannot join a movement that has rules and is organized. Regarded in that light, feminism was fine—we mostly realized we could all be feminist in our own way. The peace movements, very loose and ad hoc, have been fine. And I can work for things like Planned Parenthood or The Nature Conservancy, or a political campaign, but only as an envelope stuffer: I can't put my work directly in their service, expressing their goals. It has to follow its own course towards freedom.

Margaret: *Have you encountered any problems, publishing in the mainstream fiction world, on account of your political nature?*

Ursula: Not that I know of. It is possible that Charles Scribner, who had published my previous book and had an option on *The Dispossessed*, didn't like it because he didn't like the anarchist theme; but I think he really just thought it was a huge, boring, meaningless clunker and didn't understand it at all. He asked me to cut it by half. I said no thanks, and we broke contract amicably, and Harper & Row snapped it up—a better publisher for me then anyhow. So I can't say I have suffered for my politics.

> Fiction is not a good medium for preaching or for planning. It is really good, though, for what we used to call consciousness-raising.

SF and fantasy slip under the wire a lot, you know? People just aren't looking for radical thought in a field the respectable critics define as escapist drivel.

Some of it is escapist all right, but what it's escaping is the drivel of popular fiction and most TV and movies.

Margaret: *I feel like you do an excellent job of presenting quite radical concepts in stories that don't feel like propaganda. For example, in the story "Ile Forest" in* Orsinian Tales, *I believe you undermine the reader's faith in such ideas as codified law.*

Ursula: Hah! That pleases me! It is such a romantic story, I never thought of it as having a subversive sense, but of course you're quite right, it does.

Margaret: *I might be mistaken, but I'm under the impression that the modern fantasy/sci-fi culture intentionally shies away from politics more than it used to. A lot of magazines, for example, specifically list that they are not interested in works that deal with political issues.*

Ursula: They do? Wow. That is depressing beyond words. They're setting up their own wire.

Margaret: *Have you seen a change in this direction?*

Ursula: I am just not looking at the market any more. I haven't written short stories now for quite a while, and if I did, it would be my agent who figured where best to send them.

But maybe this is one of the reasons why I'm not reading much SF any more. I pick it up, then I put it down. Maybe I just o.d.'d on it. But it seems sort of academic, almost, lately. Doing the same stuff over fancier, more hardware, more noir. I may be totally wrong about this.

Margaret: *You've coined perhaps my favorite one-line descriptions of what an anarchist is: "One who, choosing, accepts the responsibility of choice." Would you describe yourself as an anarchist?*

Ursula: I don't, because I entirely lack the activist element, and so it seems phony or too easy. Like white people who say they are "part Cherokee."

Margaret: *I hope you don't mind that a lot of us claim you, in* *approximately the same way that we claim Tolstoy. (Who I believe can be quoted as saying "The anarchists are right ... in everything except their belief that anarchism can be reached through revolution," although I've only read this quote, and not his original essay.)*

Ursula: Of course I don't mind! I am touched and feel unworthy.

Margaret: *What were your first interactions with anarchism?*

Ursula: When I got the idea for *The Dispossessed*, the story I sketched out was all wrong, and I had to figure out what it really was about and what it needed. What it needed was first about a year of reading all the Utopias, and then another year or two of reading all the anarchist writers. That was my main interaction with anarchism. I was lucky: that stuff was hard to come by in the seventies—shadows of Sacco and Vanzetti!—but there was a very-far-left bookseller here in Portland, and if you got to know him he let you see his fine collection of all the old Anarchist writings, and some of the newer people like Bookchin too. So I got a good education.

I felt totally at home with (pacifist, not violent) anarchism, just as I always had with Taoism (they are related, at least by affinity). It is the only mode of political thinking that I do feel at home with. It also links up more and more interestingly, these days, with behavioral biology and animal psychology (as Kropotkin knew it would).

Margaret: *One book I've seen—an overview of anarchist history—attributes the first "anarchist" literature to an early Taoist thinker, and included the essay, although I can't for the life of me remember the title or author. I find the connection quite interesting, however.*

Ursula: Well, parts of Lao Tzu's book *The Tao Te Ching*, and parts of Chuang Tzu's book, which is mostly just called by his name, are clearly and radically anarchistic (and Chuang Tzu is funny, too). The best translation is by Burton Watson. I did a version of Lao Tzu which brings out the anarchism pretty clearly, and I also managed to remove the sexist language, which was fun (and not too outrageous, since ancient Chinese generally doesn't specify gender). Shambhala is the publisher. Those are the two big names in "philosophical" Taoism (i.e. not the Taoist religion, which is quite a different matter).

Margaret: *I've read an essay of yours in which you talk about gender in English, and I justed wanted to ask: when did the singular "they" fall out of written English? It's nice to be able to defend the practice.*

Ursula: Grammarians in the seventeenth and eighteenth century, trying to kind of cut a common path through the wild jungle of Elizabethan English, regularized a lot of usages—including spelling—not a bad idea in itself; but they admired Latin so much they used it as their model, rather than looking at how English actually solved some of these problems. "The reader" or "A person" doesn't agree in number with "they," and in Latin it is genuinely necessary that subject and verb agree in number, so they said it was necessary in English. (Actually it isn't always, because we have other ways of making the meaning clear, like word order, which is almost irrelevant in Latin.) So colloquial usages such as "he don't" (which my father, a professor, sometimes used) were frowned out of the written language, and so was the indefinite "they," even though it turns up in Shakespeare. But the grammarians couldn't get it out of the spoken language. It is perfectly alive and well there. "If anybody wants their ice cream they better hurry up!" So it doesn't take an awfully big jolt to just slip it back into written English.

It is funny how the people who object most furiously to "incorrectness" like that almost always turn out to be far right politically and/or socially insecure. **Ⓐ**

"Any book that doesn't
start from the fact that this
culture is killing the planet
and work to resolve that is
unforgivable. We'd be better
off with blank pages."

—Derrick Jensen

DERRICK JENSEN

My friend and I hitch-hiked down to California to interview Derrick Jensen, an author better known for his radical philosophy than for fiction. But I had read Walking on Water, *a book he wrote about writing and education, and it was one of the impetuses for this collection.*

It was a windy, rainy day in a rather dull, lifeless, stripmall sort of town, and when my friend and I spotted a small circle-A graffitied on a grocery store we immediately began to suspect Derrick. He met us and directed us to a nearly empty restaurant where we conducted our interview. I didn't work up the nerve to ask him about the graffiti. Instead, we talked about finding a publisher, language, fiction, writing, anarchism, and Dungeons & Dragons. *He even managed to bring my sex life into the conversation. Politely, mind you.*

Margaret: *Among your numerous non-fiction books, you've got one that's about creative writing,* Walking on Water. *But still, it took you years to find a publisher for your two novels. Can you tell me about how hard it was to find a publisher and why you think that was?*

Derrick: Oh, it was really hard. I would have figured that with 13 books out now, or however many, that it would easy to get my work published. I've received a boatload of awards and all of that, but it's still not easy. It's obviously easier than it was, because getting published before took years and looked impossible.

My agent sent out the novels to a bunch of publishers and they all disliked them pretty intensely. I got very negative rejection letters. So then I thought, shoot, I'll try really small anarchist presses. I did that with my zoo book [*Thought to Exist in the Wild*]. That was published by a very small press, No Voice Unheard, and they did a great job with it. But I couldn't even find an itty-bitty little press. The itty-bitty presses who thought about it were making really absurd comments. There're sections in my book *Songs of the Dead* that are about how parasites can control the behavior of their hosts, and how that's true for humans too. And one person suggested that I cut all the fiction and make it into a non-fiction book about that.

In my other book I go back and forth in time, and a publisher suggested that I make the book entirely linear and cut out half of it. That book has basically two trajectories. The book is about a person who is a paper revolutionary like me, who talks about revolution but isn't taking up weapons, and she works on toxics in the inner city. One night she's on her way home from work and she gets mugged, and she's fairly combative, and as she's getting mugged, she blurts out, "What's the difference between street thugs and corporate stooges? It makes you such a big man to beat up on me? Why do you think I'm here? I'm here to save kids from cancer." And what she doesn't know is that one of the guys, his little sister died of cancer, and it really pisses him off. Later on he goes and visits his brother in the penitentiary, and his brother says, "You know, she's right. If you take some gunpowder and you set it on fire, all you have is a stink in your house and a burn mark on your table, but if you put that gunpowder behind a bullet, you got something." And his point is direct your anger, don't just spew it at everybody.

So he shows up at her work months and months later and apologizes. It ends up that they kidnapped the CEO of the company that has toxified that part of the city. And she doesn't have a choice. She can tell him to go, in which case she's showing that everything she's ever written is just rhetoric, or she can participate in a capital crime. That's the main story. They wanted me to only keep that, and they wanted me to cut the other story that talks about what happens to her life after that night. I've got them interspersed. I didn't want to make that cut.

And finally I found PM Press. I'm very happy with them so far. They published my interview book [*How Shall I Live My Life?*], and they did my most recent CD [*Now This War Has Two Sides*], and now they're doing these two novels, one of which will be out within a couple of weeks, *Songs of the Dead*.

Margaret: *It seems like there's a kind of a stigma against publishing fiction in the radical political scene, and there are people who just think it's frivolous when compared to theory, like the people who wanted to cut your book down to just theory.*

Derrick: I think that the people who think that fiction is frivolous have a really good point, actually. I think the problem isn't with the theorists or the people who would look down their noses at fiction; I think that the problem is with a lot of modern fiction.

A great example of that: I was watching this awful, awful movie a few months ago, called *The Diving Bell and the Butterfly*. It's a movie that's based on this memoir. It's a memoir of this guy who has a stroke and when he wakes up after having the stroke he's in the hospital and can only move his left eye. He finally figures out a language he can use, with the help of a nurse, and he then dictates his memoir to this nurse. And he's a horrible person. Before he did this he was the editor of some fashion magazine in Paris, and the whole memoir is incredibly pitying. What he wants to say to his children is, "Now you know what it's like to have a monster for a father." He has nothing to say.

I'm watching this movie, and I'm just hating it, and I'm thinking that it seemed really familiar. And I realized it was basically the plot of the book *Johnny Got His Gun* [by Dalton Trumbo], which is one of the best anti-war books ever written. And that's about a soldier who wakes up in bed and slowly realizes that he's lost his eyes, nose, mouth, ears, arms, legs, he's lost everything. During the book, he figures out how to communicate by pushing his head against the pillow, and he then dictates this extraordinary anti-capitalist manifesto. It's the opposite thing... we have the same plot, but *The Diving Bell and the Butterfly* says nothing.

> One of the big complaints that almost every publisher had about my novels is that I was attempting to make philosophical and political points. Both are about fighting back.

Just last night I was at my mom's watching *Oliver Twist* on Masterpiece Theatre, and Charles Dickens, he was making some extraordinarily powerful points about the poor. And you take Émile Zola, who wrote *Germinal*, a lot of those writers understood that, like Bertolt Brecht said, "Art is not a mirror with which to reflect life, but rather a hammer with which to shape it." And yet one of the big complaints that almost every publisher had about my novels is that I was attempting to make philosophical and political points. Both are about fighting back.

Fiction has really lost its way. If you write fiction that makes important points, then suddenly you're preaching. And having said that, I have to tell you, I've read some really shitty novels by people who had points to say but they weren't good enough at fiction. Those are different skill sets, theorizing and writing fiction. But there are some novelists who are making really good points. You know who is actually writing books about killing those who are killing the natural world? Karl Hiaasen, with his really silly adventure novels. Developers and stuff end up being fed to alligators.

I think that part of the problem is that modern fiction, a lot of it, *is* meaningless. And I think that that's a huge, huge problem with fiction, and not with the anarchist theorists.

Margaret: *I've been researching the political associations of a lot of the old writers I used to read, the classics. Finding out that Camus wrote for anarchist papers... and when Sacco and Vanzetti were on trial, all of the literary world spoke up for them. But where is the literary world with Eric McDavid?*

Derrick: I have a story about this... I'm not going to name the person, but it's an important story. I was talking to a writer once, who has written very eloquently about protecting certain places and/or creatures. I was talking to this person, who said that he had gotten a call from an environmental organization that wanted him to lend his name in an effort to protect this place or creature he had written about. This was weeks or months before, and when he was talking to me he was furious, he was saying, "I'm a writer, not an activist, and I'm losing my objectivity." And I was so pissed off. That's outrageous. That's the same old thing of *using* the animals or that place and not giving back. And obviously I have spoken out in defense of Eric McDavid and others, and I'm not saying that because, "Oh, I'm so great." I'm saying that because it really pisses me off that other artists don't do that.

Margaret: *It seems like the people who actually made the changes in the artistic world were aware of the political na-*

*ture of everything and, while they might not have been ob-
sessed with politics—although some of them certainly were
and that tends to be forgotten—they didn't shy away from
them either.*

Derrick: One thing a lot of people forget, as I say over and
over in *Endgame*, is that all writing is propaganda. Sometimes, for example, I'll go over to my mom's and watch a
BBC mystery or something. It's embarrassing that I really
like them, because all they are is pro-police-state propaganda. It's all about how cops get it right. That doesn't alter the
fact that it's a good story. I get caught up in the story and
I'm like, "Oh! Catch the criminals! Oh, wait, I don't want
the criminals caught." The point is that, whether a story is
political or not, it's political.

If I can make a recommendation—I haven't read this since
my twenties, so it might not be as good as I remember—
there's an essay that was called "On Moral Fiction" by John
Gardner. In there, he talks about exactly what we're talking
about, about how previously writers wrote something, and
now so often they don't. I mean, you write what you know—
like in *Germinal*, it's a very good book. Nihilists don't end
up looking good in it, but it's a really good book about the
horrible conditions in mines in France. And there's a scene
where I just couldn't stop sobbing, about this horse that is
taken down into the mine when he's a little foal and then he
is never brought up again. And what happens is that he lives
his life down in the mine and at some point the mine gets
flooded and the horse is desperately trying to get away and
can't. The author actually went to mines and walked around
in them and that's how he learned that.

Gardner also points out—and this is so true and it makes
me sick—that there are so many novels today about being a
college professor and being in therapy and fucking students.

You know why? Because the fucking author is a college professor who is in therapy who is fucking students. So no wonder a lot of writers don't write about activism: a lot of writers aren't activists.

Margaret: *How did you get involved in writing, and specifically in teaching writing?*

Derrick: I always wanted to be a writer ever since I was a kid. The thing is, when I was in high school, I went through calculus, and I got accepted with a full ride scholarship to an engineering school. And if you get through calculus in high school and you get a full ride scholarship to an engineering school, then you're insane if you want to go be a writer. I tried to transfer at some point and the registrar at where I wanted to transfer actually said to me: "you have a full ride scholarship and you want to transfer here? Are you insane?" Because when I got out of engineering school, I would have started at 35 or 40k back in 1983. Honestly, at this point I've still never made anything close to 35 or 40k. It's the big cliché, and I'm sure you know this: writing is a great way to make a life and a terrible way to make a living. So if you presume that money is what's important then you'd be an idiot to be a writer. Even though I didn't really like science, didn't like math.

I was miserable in college and I realized I didn't want to wake up when I was 65 and go, "who the hell's life was this?" So I realized that I would do whatever it took to be a writer. Then I spent my twenties... if you're going to look at this from a production standpoint, I spent my twenties doing nothing, if you're going to look at this from a soul stand- He said to me: "You have been given gifts. Your ability to write is a gift. And if the universe gives you gifts and you don't use them in service to your community, then you're not worth shit."

point, I spent my twenties getting grounded. But that sounds a lot more hoity-toity than it actually was: what it actually was is that I spent a lot of time sitting by a river, which once again sounds really enlightened and everything but it's not. I sat by the river and then I went home and watched the Cubs. I spent a lot of time doing nothing.

My mom was very supportive of that, but my mom doesn't have any patience for people who are lazy. She just trusted me. How did she know that I was just going to waste 4 or 5 years figuring out who I was as opposed to just being a lazy person who was going to waste my life? Which is not to say that a person has to be productive; I think that it's really important for people to vomit up the effects of their schooling and to teach themselves how to think, to teach themselves how to write, to teach themselves what is important, and to teach themselves how to feel. All of those things are really important and it can take a really long time and I have a lot of patience for that process, in myself and others, and for people spending a lot of time confused. The thing that I don't have patience for is for people who are just sort of... I don't have a lot of patience for laziness. How do you know? I've had some friends that I think obviously have some issues, that they have tremendous talent and they're never going to fulfill that talent because they are too lazy to do that work, or they have emotional issues or low self-esteem, any combination.

> Nobody's going to give a shit as to what good books we wrote, or whether we did treesits or didn't do treesits. What they're going to care about is whether they can breathe the air and drink the water. The land is everything.

I remember, an important point came to me when I was 27. I called this friend of mine, and he gave me this lecture. If he had done it sooner it would have bugged the hell out of me but, as it was, it was perfect. He said to me, "You have been given gifts. Your ability to write is a gift. And if the universe gives you gifts and you don't use them in service to your community, then you're not worth shit." And that's where I really fall on the whole laziness line, that if you've got some gifts, you damn well better use 'em, you better repay the universe for giving you those gifts. It's like caterpillars and butterflies: you've gotta go through this period of pupation, and you have to go through this, and that's what my twenties were, this period of pupation where I was becoming no longer the person I was as a teenager and becoming the person I am as an adult. And perhaps that process would have gone faster for me had I been in a functioning community that could have told me that this is the process I was going through as opposed to me just knowing that I was miserable? I mean, I didn't like myself, I didn't like my life, I didn't like anything.

There's a great line by Herman Hesse, in *Demian*: "I wanted only to act according to the promptings that came from my true self, why was that so very difficult?"

Oh I gotta tell you this. I was doing a talk in Los Angeles several years ago. And these parents had brought their 14 year-old daughter, and she was this total fan. It was in this church, and it was this little talk, actually it was more of a discussion than a lecture, and then she started talking about, "What should I do with my life?" I'm not really saying anything, I'm just listening to her talk. This is after the sort of big Q&A and now there's like 15 of us sorta sitting around. This was so great because she was sitting there, and her parents were sitting behind her. And she's just rambling like a 14 year-old would do, and then at one point she says, "Maybe what I should do is find what I love to do, and then do it again."

And then I said, "I'm sorry, I didn't hear what you said, could you say it again?" And then she said it again. And I said, "The acoustics in here are really bad because I still can't hear you. Can you say it again?" And then she said it again. And I said, "God, it's really weird, because I'm still not understanding, can you say it again?" and she said it again. It was great cause I still remember her parents eyes were just shining with tears, and I had her say it again and again... She obviously figured out what was going on pretty quick. But I mean, that's it. Figuring out what you love to do, and then doing it again.

And that's sort of the short version, believe it or not, of how I became a writer.

Margaret: *You mentioned that writing is a sort of a gift that you need to use in service of the community...*

Derrick: For me, if someone else knows explosives, they should use that. I mean, whatever. That's the thing, I've gotten a bunch of emails from people over the years, it bugs the shit out of me. I've gotten probably ten. Organizers saying, "You know, you've written enough. Now you should organize." I was thinking, "Jesus Christ, I'm not an organizer." That's not my gift. I'm terrible at that. I mean, I'm not really a people person—most writers aren't. If I was social, I wouldn't be a writer. So whatever your gifts are.

Margaret: *What do you feel like you can accomplish through your writing to serve your community? Have you seen anything specific and tangible?*

Derrick: Well, there's still dams standing, so obviously my work isn't doing what I want. I've gotten bazillions of notes from people, and the most common type of note I get is saying, "I thought I was the only one who was thinking these things, that civilization is unsustainable, and that it's insane, that working in a wage job is insane," or, "I thought I was the only person who thought that zoos are insane. So thank you for letting me know that I'm not alone." And that's really gratifying and that makes me really happy. And I've gotten so many notes from people, geez, I've gotten notes from women who've—men have never done this, oddly enough— I've gotten notes from women who've divorced their abusive husbands they say because of my books. Obviously they were ready for it. There're people who've become activists because of it, there's all sorts of stuff. And that's really great.

The bottom line is, how does it help the land? Does it? I don't know. This is something I say in *Endgame*, I say in my talks, you know nobody's going to give a shit as to what good books we wrote, or whether we did treesits or didn't do treesits, or whether we recycled, or whether we were vegetarians or not vegetarians, or whether the potstickers [which we were eating] were any good, they're not going to care about any of that. What they're

I'm not sure that the world needs more descriptions of beautiful places. Look out your fucking back door, ya know? What we need is to stop this culture from killing the planet.

going to care about is whether they can breathe the air and drink the water. The land is everything. And so, is my work helping to save the salmon? I don't know. And that's a tremendous source of frustration.

As a writer you are, by definition, abstracted, from the real work. There are layers between you—even when I affect somebody and let them know that they're not alone—there're still those layers.

So what do I want, is your question? What do I want to accomplish?

Margaret: *What do you feel like can be accomplished through writing, in the sense of the health of the landbase, etc.?*

Derrick: I'm doing a conference, I hate conferences, but I'm doing a conference next week actually, in South Carolina, and it's a conference of nature writing or something. And the reason I'm doing it is because *Orion* published an excerpt of *Endgame* that really helped jumpstart the book, and they have a lot to do with it, so I'm doing it basically as a favor to them. One of the things I'm going to talk about is... basically, for years, I was going to write an essay called "Why I can't read nature writing," cause I hate most nature writing. One of the reasons I hate it is because I'm not sure that the world needs more descriptions of beautiful places. Look out your fucking back door, ya know? What we *need* is to stop this culture from killing the planet.

I'm writing a book right now with Eric McBay, about shit, about decay, and basically the book is about how this culture has taken shit, which is a beautiful gift to the landbase, and turned it into a toxic thing. In nature, somebody's shit is somebody else's food. There is no waste in nature. You've seen, I'm sure, that there's 6 times as much plastic as phytoplankton in the ocean. This culture's creating these... I mean, how long is this [*points to a plastic water cup*] going to be here, or this [*points to my recorder*]? And I'm not picking on you; I've got a truck, and a computer, and blah blah blah. For crying out loud, how long is this [*grabs the tablecloth*] going to last? I don't know if it's made of polyester or if it's made of cotton. And it's an interesting book because I've always been fascinated by decay; it's really fun, you know, all these fun facts about shit and fungus and everything else. But a problem Eric and I were having with it, one of the things that I've been thinking about a lot as I've been writing this book ... R.D. Laing, in his book *The Politics of Experience* had the best first line ever of any book, which is: "Few books today are forgivable." The whole book is about alienation, how we're so horribly desperately alienated. The point is if your book doesn't start with this alienation as your starting point, and work towards resolving it, insofar as any piece of writing can resolve alienation, which is a big question, then it's not forgivable and you'd be better off with blank pages. Basically in this book, I'm saying that any book that doesn't start from the fact that this culture is killing the planet and work to resolve that is unforgivable. We'd be better off with blank pages.

So what do I want to accomplish with my writing? I want to bring down civilization, I want to stop this culture from killing the planet. And writing is my gift, and writing is my weapon, and if it ends up that writing isn't a good enough weapon I'll have to choose another weapon. Because, and this is what I'm going to say next week, is that so many nature writers forget that writing is a means to an end. Maybe if the planet weren't being killed then we'd all have the luxury of just writing fun little stories, that it doesn't matter if it's a fun little story about a vampire or a fun little story about the beautiful bird out your window. It doesn't matter. Right now we don't have that luxury. And that's a question I think about every day. How does my work help to bring down civilization?

Margaret: *What are your associations with anarchism, and would you describe yourself as an anarchist? How did you get interested in it?*

Derrick: I get called an anarchist a lot. I think that's the most accurate way to say it, I get called an anarchist a lot, and I don't mind. Do I self identify as an anarchist? Sometimes. It's a label. Like any other label, I guess I'll use it when it feels right, and I won't use it when it doesn't feel right. I'll tell you, this review I got one time, it's so funny. I don't remember what magazine it was in, someone was attacking me for not being enough of an anarchist. How can you be not enough of an anarchist? Isn't that a contradiction? Do we have rules?

This one anarchist actually told me this joke: "If there's a party, how do you recognize the anarchists? They're the ones all wearing the same uniform." I read a really good book, *History of Anarchism*, and the author took anarchism back to Lao-tzu, back to the cynics in Greece. If I can use his definition... I don't remember his definition. If I can use his lineage of anarchism, I'm down for anarchism. If I go with some of its other manifestations, then I'm probably not. I got interviewed for *Green Anarchy* a few years ago. They started the interview by asking me if I'm a green anarchist. And I said, "You know? I don't give a shit. If you want to call me that that's great, but what I really care about is living in a world that has wild salmon, and living in a world that has no dioxin in a mothers breast milk, a world that has icecaps, whatever, and if that makes me a green anarchist, great, if it makes me not a green anarchist, great." It's the same with anarchism.

I have problems with labels anyway. I mean, it took me years before I'd call myself a writer. People would say, "What are you," and I'd say, "I'm a person." That felt really precious to me. So yeah, I'm a writer, I'm an anarchist, I'm an anarcho-primitivist, whatever you want to call me, whatever, but then I'm a capitalist for that matter; I mean, I sell books, I have a little publishing company. So yeah, I'm a capitalist and damn proud of it. Whatever. It's all just... once again John Zerzan's thought has been very important to me, I like John. Do you know John at all?

Margaret: *I don't know him personally.*

Derrick: He and I, we've been friends for ten years or something. And for ten years we've been having this great disagreement about the degree to which symbolic representation is always alienating. And it's just, if anarchism consists of conversations like that, then yeah, sure, it's wonderful, respectful, it's the way I wish every disagreement was. Each of us is very respectful of the other's position, and each of us respects the other's work, and we still have some disagreements that we don't hold back on expressing.

Margaret: *That was actually my next question, about primitivism and anti-language and mediation. And I was going to say that one of the reasons I feel like more people connect with your work than the other primitivist theory; it doesn't say, by using words that I have to look up in a dictionary, that I can't use language. Because I think that a critique of mediation, an awareness of mediation, and how, yeah, there's barriers between people and your work when they read it, I think that all of that is very important...*

Derrick: Right. Well, that's another thing, John Zerzan says if we're sitting in a restaurant and it catches on fire, then it would be nice if one of us said to the other one, "You know, it's on fire, we need to leave." There is a place for language. The thing that helped resolve for me the question of whether language is inherently alienating... I mean, it's a no-brainer. So you two [*indicating my friend and I*] are lovers?

Margaret: *Yeah.*

Derrick: So if I say, "Lips touching, tongues touching, kissing in the ear, whispering in the ear," then it's different than them happening, and they have a different effect. Obviously words are not actions, and so in that sense they are inherently alienating. I mean, I can write up this really passionate sexy scene, and it's still just ink on paper. Likewise I can write this really horrible scene like the introduction to *Culture of Make Believe*.

One day I was driving and I pulled off the interstate, and there was a stop sign on the offramp. And I suddenly got it. The stop sign doesn't stop your car, the stop sign tells you to stop your car. And so I suddenly understand.

Joseph Campbell said this about the people who literally believe the Bible: "You don't go to a restaurant and eat the menu. The menu is telling you something else, the menu is pointing to something." So as long as we recognize that me saying, "There's a fire over there" is not the fire itself, then there shouldn't a problem. The problem comes—and this is a real problem in this culture, because people are insane—when we confuse what is real and what is not real, or when other people do, and so they confuse the words for the reality. That's when it becomes a problem. This is part of a much bigger problem. I see this with all the so-called solutions to global warming; they all take industrial civilization and industrial capitalism as a given, and the natural world as secondary. So basically, it's how can we maintain this culture, and it would be nice if we still have a world. But what's primary are those trees out there, the rain. That's what's real, everything else is negotiable. Does that make sense?

> Stories are how we learn how to be human beings. And if the stories you see routinely show people like you committing acts of violence and getting away with it, you're going to be different than if stories routinely show you being victimized.

Margaret: *Yeah. You mention in* Endgame *that you used to play* Dungeons & Dragons. *Do you think that fantasy, the creation of imaginary worlds, has played a role in your po-litical/social development? We play D&D, is the reason we ask.*

Derrick: One thing, I don't think this answers your question, one thing that I learned didn't have to do with activism. It was an existential question. If my character would die, then I'd just roll up another one. I was never one of those people who would kill themselves when their character died. We were all just like, "Okay I didn't like him anyway, let's roll up another one. God, this one is really stupid and really weak and really not charismatic. Okay I'll send him in to get killed." And one time I was rolling up a character after having yet another one die, and I realized, you know, this is the end. This isn't a big deal for me, but if this character were alive, then this character would be dead. And I suddenly realized that it's the same for me. It's like, okay, I've been given these gifts by the universe, and I'm going to die some day, and I'm not going to get rewards. So far as I know, when I die I'm done, so I need to live my life to the fullest. I need to be what I want to be, to explore those gifts. So that was the lesson it really taught me.

I don't think it taught me anything as an activist. In retrospect, the lessons of *Dungeons & Dragons*, I don't know if it's any better now, they're appalling, they're so pro-civ. So basically, lawful is a good thing, that means you obey the rules. Why are orcs and kobolds the bad guys? All of these various creatures who are just living their lives, what are they called? Ochre jelly?

Margaret: *Yeah, and the gelatinous cube.*

Derrick: Yeah. It's just hanging out, it's not hurting anybody, and we see anything like that, giant slugs, you gotta kill 'em. You gotta kill everything you see. The lessons were pretty appalling, in retrospect. Another thing I thought is pretty interesting about *Dungeons & Dragons*, I thought it would be a pretty darn good psychological evolution tool. A lot of the people I played with, some of them might be real sadists. When we start playing, they devise all these nasty, extraordinary tortures. It's like, "I guess I understand you a bit better now, don't I?"

Margaret: *Have you run into any impediments in publishing because of your status as a radical, of how far you take your words?*

Derrick: I think the question is, "Have I ever *not* run into impediments to getting stuff published." Yes, I've run into those impediments. I was actually surprised they published *Endgame*. I'm lucky; no publisher has ever tried to censor me, no publisher has ever tried to take the edge off my work. I've heard so many stories of other writers who have been censored. Of course I'm also going with small publishers who don't give me big advances, but I'm very pleased with my publishers in that way. I don't know if you know this, but the rule in publishing is that the writer has final say over all of the words and the publisher has final say over things like the cover, the title and marketing. So if they were to say, "I want you to cut this," I would say, "I will listen to your arguments," and they always recognize that I have the final say.

I really like my agent right now. He's great, his politics are very radical obviously. And he doesn't tell me to edit my stuff. I've fired agents before. I had one agent that read the first 70 pages of *Language* and told me that if I took out the social criticism and the family stuff, I'd have a book. I fired her. I've had agents, early on in my career, try to stifle me, try to "steer me towards bigger audiences." Sierra Club didn't take the zoo book because they thought it was too much of a rant. They said that it wouldn't help animals at all.

I think my fiction writing is good, I don't think that that's why it hasn't gotten not accepted anywhere. Part of it is the idea. If you have a book where someone kidnaps and kills a CEO, that's totally different than if you have a book where somebody kidnaps and kills a woman. That's every movie that's on HBO right now, that's what you do.

It's what George Gerber talked about: casting and fate. George Gerber was the TV violence guy; he studied violence from the '50s 'til 2005, when he died. And when people talk about how much violence is on TV, they're citing his studies. I interviewed him, he's a great guy. He said everybody gets his stuff wrong, they always misinterpret him. His problem is not that there's violence on TV, he doesn't care about that, or movies, his problem is that he says that violence is a social relation, and the question is who does what to whom. He studied how many times in movies men commit acts of violence, versus how many times do women commit acts of violence, and who is doing them. What he found, no surprise, is that white males, on film and TV and movies, commit violence with impunity, and if a woman commits an act of violence, then the whole movie has to be about why she would do something so disturbing. But Bruce Willis? Kills somebody in the first three minutes. And that's really important because what he says is, these are stories. I mean, there's this great line by a Scottish balladeer: "If I could write all the ballads, I wouldn't care who wrote the laws." And it's so true because stories are how we learn—we are for better or worse social creatures—and stories are how we learn how to be human beings. And if the stories you see routinely show people like you committing acts of violence and getting away with it,

All the so-called solutions to global warming take industrial civilization and industrial capitalism as a given, and the natural world as secondary. So basically, it's how can we maintain this culture, and it would be nice if we still have a world. But what's primary are those trees out there, the rain. That's what's real, everything else is negotiable.

you're going to be different than if stories routinely show you being victimized. That's a really important thing. Why'd I bring that up? What was your question?

Margaret: *Impediments...*

Derrick: That's one of the things that I think, is that it's distasteful for many people to have a book where a woman, of all people, kills a CEO. People have said, "Oh my god, your books are so violent," but that's not true at all. The body count on my books is much lower than your standard Hollywood movie. The thing I've found really important is that I bring meaning to it. And the problem is, if you put meaning and violence together? Nature writers can say, "Oh, it's so terrible" and philosophers can use big words to say, "Oh, it's so terrible" and then you can have this huge body count in a movie. But the problem is, if you put a body count together with the analysis, it's not additive but multiplicative, do you see what I'm trying to say?

Frankly, I've known a lot of "anarchists" for whom it was basically an excuse to be irresponsible, and to be fuckups.

Margaret: *When I was talking to Ursula Le Guin about it, she mentioned that fiction was good for what people used to call consciousness raising, creating a culture... I feel like that's one thing that your work has contributed to.*

Derrick: One of the reasons I don't bother to learn primitive living skills is that I'm not going to survive the crash. Either those in power will kill me... Somebody asked John Stockwell, "If everything you say about the CIA is true, then why are you still alive?" "Because they're winning." And so I'm safe for now. I can say whatever I want, they don't give a shit. But if they start to lose, we're all dead. And one's purity and one's silence won't save you. Those in power will do what it takes to maintain power.

That's one thing, the other thing is that Crohn's Disease will kill me. So I'm dead through the crash. But that's okay because if the big revolution comes that I've been working for my whole professional life, my whole personal life at this point, if that came, I'd be done anyway, my work's done. My work is about creating culture where what I'm writing about can take place. And once it starts, my work takes a long time... Jesus, if I finished a book today, it doesn't come out for at least a year. There's a big time lag, and then after that, people have to read it, people have to digest it, they have to internalize it, they have metabolize it, they have to shit out what they don't accept, and they have to turn what they do accept into theirs, and that takes years. And so my role is really a longer term thing. There's this great movie, *The Battle of Algiers*. Have you seen it?

Margaret *No, but I've heard it was required viewing for the Black Panthers.*

Derrick: It's also required viewing at West Point. It's *the* movie on insurgency and anti-insurgency. And I was thinking about where I would fit into the movie. It's about an insurgency against the French in Algeria, and where I would fit into this movie is that my books would be on the shelves of the people who are doing the fighting. That doesn't mean I don't have other roles; I spent most of the day today fighting a timber harvest plan. But what I'm really trying to do is lay a philosophical and emotional and intellectual groundwork for all of this. When *Listening to the Land* came out, Barry Lopez read the first line: "We are members of the most destructive culture ever to exist," then he held it at arm's length and said, "This is great, somebody is finally saying it." And that's what I do: I finally say the stuff that a lot of people are thinking. And yeah, I see my role the same as Ursula K. Le Guin's in that way. She has one of my favorite lines ever about writing, which is, "Writing is a lot like sex, it's better with two people." It's one thing to write in a journal, and it's another to write for an audience. It's an interactive thing, and a lot of people don't understand that and a lot of people's writing ends up being essentially journal writing that someone else is supposed to read. It's like, "Why the fuck am I supposed to read this? It's boring as hell." And I really like the way she puts that because it's essentially like masturbating with another person. It's like, "Hi I'm here, I'm having a great time, you don't exist, but I don't care." Which is of course the patriarchal model. Tell her I think her work has been really vital.

Margaret: *She also wrote possibly my favorite line about anarchism: "An anarchist is one who, given the choice, chooses responsibility." [I misquoted her slightly. My apologies.]*

Derrick: That's great, under that definition, yeah, I'll call myself an anarchist. One of the problems I've had with a lot of anarchists, is that frankly, I've known a lot of "anarchists" for whom it was basically an excuse to be irresponsible, and to be fuckups.

I got into this little argument with these kids several years ago. They were saying that anarchism is about doing whatever you want whenever you want to do it. I said, you know, let's say we're all going to do an action. And you decide at the last minute that you don't feel like doing it tonight, you're going to watch a movie, you're going to stay at home and smoke pot. And because you don't show up, the action fails and my brother dies. I'm gonna kill you. Because my brother is dead because of you, because you chose to stay home and smoke pot. There has to accountability if we're going to have any sort of real movement, there has to be discipline. The truth is I would want to vet him out beforehand, so I wouldn't get in the position where I was relying on him in the first place. Ⓐ

"I believe that all other political states are in fact variations or outgrowths of a basic state of anarchy; after all, when you mention the idea of anarchy to most people they will tell you what a bad idea it is because the biggest gang would just take over. Which is pretty much how I see contemporary society."

—Alan Moore

ALAN MOORE

I first heard of Alan Moore as the author of V for Vendetta, *the graphic novel that pits an anarchist hero against a tyrannical British government. And then I heard more and more about him. He transformed D.C. Comics'* Swampthing *into an eco-warrior. He wrote* Watchmen, *often considered the finest graphic novel ever written. He rebirthed Steampunk with* The League of Extraordinary Gentlemen. *He also, by the way, adamantly does not stand by the movies that were filmed of his works (*From Hell, V for Vendetta, The League of Extraordinary Gentlemen*). But since most of his work in his younger years was for major comics publishers, he owns very little of his own work.*

An acquaintance passed along his phone number, and I called him at his home in Britain. He spoke eloquently of politics, history, and the impact of fiction upon our lives.

Margaret: *I'll start with the basics: What are your associations with anarchism? Do you consider yourself an anarchist? How did you first get involved in radical politics?*

Alan: Well I suppose I first got involved in radical politics as a matter of course, during the late 1960s when it was a part of the culture. The counterculture, as we called it then, was very eclectic and all-embracing. It included fashions of dress, styles of music, philosophical positions, and, inevitably, political positions. And although there would be various political leanings coming to the fore from time to time, I suppose that the overall consensus political standpoint was probably an anarchist one. Although probably back in those days, when I was a very young teenager, I didn't necessarily put it into those terms. I was probably not familiar enough with the concepts of anarchy to actually label myself as such. It was later, as I went into my twenties and started to think about things more seriously that I came to a conclusion that basically the only political standpoint that I could possibly adhere to would be an anarchist one.

It furthermore occurred to me that, basically, anarchy is in fact the only political position that is actually possible. I believe that all other political states are in fact variations or outgrowths of a basic state of anarchy; after all, when you mention the idea of anarchy to most people they will tell you what a bad idea it is because the biggest gang would just take over. Which is pretty much how I see contemporary society.

> You are trying to express your own view of reality and existence, and that is inevitably going to be a political action.

We live in a badly developed anarchist situation in which the biggest gang has taken over and have declared that it is not an anarchist situation—that it is a capitalist or a communist situation. But I tend to think that anarchy is the most natural form of politics for a human being to actually practice. All it means, the word, is no leaders. *An-archon.* No leaders.

And I think that if we actually look at nature without prejudice, we find that this is the state of affairs that usually pertains. I mean, previous naturalists have looked at groups of animals and have said, "Ah, yes, this animal is the alpha male, so he is the leader of the group." Whereas later research tends to suggest that this is simply the researcher projecting his own social visions onto a group of animals, and that if you observe them more closely you will find out that, yes, there is this big tough male that seems to handle most of the fights, but that the most important member of the herd is probably this female at the back that everybody seems to gather around during any conflict. There are other animals within the herd that might have an importance in terms of finding new territory. In fact, the herd does not actually structure itself in terms of hierarchies; every animal seems to have its own position within the herd.

And actually, if you look at most natural human groupings of people, such as a family or a group of friends, you will find that again, we don't have leaders. Unless you're talking about some incredibly rigid Victorian family, there is nobody that could be said to be the leader of the family; everybody has their own function. And it seems to me that anarchy is the state that most naturally obtains when you're talking about ordinary human beings living their lives in a natural way. It's only when you get these fairly alien structures of order that are represented by our major political schools of thought, that you start to get these terrible problems arising—problems regarding our status within the hierarchy, the uncertainties and insecurities that are the result of that. You get these jealousies, these power struggles, which by and large, don't really afflict the rest of the animal kingdom. It seems to me that the idea of leaders is an unnatural one that was probably thought up by a leader at some point in antiquity; leaders have been brutally enforcing that idea ever since, to the point where most people cannot conceive of an alternative.

This is one of the things about anarchy: if we were to take out all the leaders tomorrow, and put them up against a wall and shoot them—and it's a lovely thought, so let me just dwell on that for a moment before I dismiss it—but if we were to do that, society would probably collapse, because the majority of people have had thousands of years of being conditioned to depend upon leadership from a source outside themselves. That has become a crutch to an awful lot of people, and if you were to simply kick it away, then those people would simply fall over and take society with them. In order for any workable and realistic state of anarchy to be achieved, you will obviously have to educate people—and educate them massively—towards a state where they could actually take responsibility for their own actions and simultaneously be aware that they are acting in a wider group, that they must allow other people within that group to take responsibility for their own actions. Which, on a small scale, as it works in families or in groups of friends, doesn't seem to be that implausible, but it would take an awful lot of education to get people to think about living their lives in that way. And obviously, no government, no state, is ever going to educate people to the point where the state itself would become irrelevant. So if people are going to be educated to the point where they can take responsibility for their own laws and their own actions and become, to my mind, fully actualized human beings, then it will have to come from some source other than the state or government.

There have been underground traditions, both underground political traditions and underground spiritual traditions. There have been people such as John Bunyan, who spent almost 30 years in prison in nearby Bedford. This is the author of "The Pilgrim's Progress" who spent nearly 30 years in prison because the spiritual ideas he was espousing were so incendiary. This was a part of a movement; around the seventeenth century in England there were all sorts of strange ideas bubbling to the surface, particularly around the area where I live, in the midlands. You've got all of these religions—although they were often considered heretical— which were stating that there was no need for priests, that there was no need for leaders; they were hoping to announce a nation of saints. That everybody would become a saint, and that they would become mechanistic philosophers. People could work all day, as say a tinker, but that in the evening they could stand up and preach the word of the Lord with as much authority as any person in a pulpit. This looks to be a glorious idea, but you can see how it would have terrified the authorities at the time.

And indeed it was during the seventeenth century that, partly fueled by similar ideas, Oliver Cromwell rose up and commenced the British civil war, which eventually led to the beheading of Charles I. I mean it was, in the phrase of one of the best books about the period, "literally a case of the world turned upside down." There have been these underground traditions, whether they are spiritual or purely political, that have expressed anarchist ideas for centuries, and these days there is even more potential for the dissemination of ideas like that. With the growth of the internet and the growth of communication in general, these ideas are much harder to suppress. Simply putting John Bunyan in jail for 30 years isn't really going to cut it anymore. Also, the internet does suggest possibilities for throwing off centralized state control.

It struck me that simple capitalism and communism were not the two poles around which the whole of political thinking revolved. It struck me that two much more representative extremes were to be found in fascism and anarchy.

There was a very interesting piece, a 10 minute television broadcast, made over here by a gentleman from the London School of Economics, a lecturer who looked like the least threatening man that you can imagine. He didn't look like an apocalyptic political firebrand by any means; he looked like and was an accountant and an economist. And yet the actual picture he was painting was quite compelling. He was saying that the only reason that governments are governments is that they control the currency; they don't actually do anything for us that we don't pay for, other than expose us to the threat of foreign wars by their reckless actions. They don't actually really even govern us; all they do is control the currency and rake off the proceeds.

Now in the past, if you wanted to get yourself thrown into jail forever then the best way of going about it would have been not to have molested children or gone on a serial killing spree or something like that, the best way would have been to try to establish your own currency. Because the nature of currency is a kind of magic: these pieces of metal or pieces of paper only have value as long as people believe that they do. If somebody were to introduce another kind of piece of metal or piece of paper, and if people were to start believing in that form of currency more than yours, then all of your wealth would suddenly vanish. So attempts to introduce alternative currencies in the past have been ruthlessly stamped out. And with the internet, that is no longer anywhere near as easy. In fact, a lot of modern companies have rewards schemes; supermarkets run reward schemes that are in certain senses like a form of currency. A lot of companies have schemes in which workers will be paid in credits which can be redeemed from almost anything from a house to a tin of beans at the company store. There are also green economies that are starting up here and there whereby you'll have say, an underprivileged place in England where you have an out-of-work mechanic who wants his house decorated. He will, as an out-of-work mechanic, have accumulated green credits by doing the odd job around the neighborhood—fixing people's cars, stuff like that—and he will be able to spend those credits by getting in touch with an out-of-work decorator who will come and paint his house for him.

Now again, schemes like this are increasingly difficult to control, and what this lecturer from the London School of Economics was saying is that in the future we would have to be prepared for a situation in which we have firstly, no currency, and secondly, as a result of that, no government. So there are ways in which technology itself and the ways in which we respond to technology—the ways in which we adapt our culture and our way of living to accommodate breakthroughs and movements in technology—*might* give us a way to move around government. To evolve around government to a point where such a thing is no longer necessary or desirable. That is perhaps an optimistic vision, but it's one of the only realistic ways I can see it happening.

I don't believe that a violent revolution is ever going to work, simply on the grounds that it never has in the past. I mean, speaking as a resident of Northampton, during the English civil war we backed Cromwell—we provided all the boots for his army—and we were a center of antiroyalist sentiment. Incidentally, we provided all the boots to the Confederates as well, so obviously we know how to pick a winner. Cromwell's revolution? I guess it succeeded. The king was beheaded, which was quite early in the day for beheading; amongst the European monarchy, I think we can claim to have kicked off that trend. But give it another ten years; as it turned out, Cromwell himself was a monster. He was every bit the monster that Charles I had been. In some ways he was worse. When Cromwell died, the restoration happened. Charles II came to power and was so pissed off with the people of Northampton that he pulled down our castle. And the status quo was restored. I really don't think that a violent revolution is ever going to provide a long-term solution to the problems of the ordinary person. I think that is something that we had best handle ourselves, and which we are most likely to achieve by the simple evolution of western society. But that might take quite a while, and whether we have that amount of time is, of course, open to debate.

So I suppose that those are my principal thoughts upon anarchy. They've been with me for a long time. Way back in the early eighties, when I was first kicking off writing *V for Vendetta* for the English magazine *Warrior*, the story was very much a result of me actually sitting down and thinking about what the real extreme poles of politics were. Because it struck me that simple capitalism and communism were not the two poles around which the whole of political thinking revolved. It struck me that two much more representative extremes were to be found in fascism and anarchy.

We most often predicate our real lives upon fictions that we have applied from somewhere.

Fascism is a complete abdication of personal responsibility. You are surrendering all responsibility for your own actions to the state in the belief that in unity there is strength, which was the definition of fascism represented by the original Roman symbol of the bundle of bound twigs. Yes, it is a very persuasive argument: "In unity there is strength." But inevitably people tend to come to a conclusion that the bundle of bound twigs will be much stronger if all the twigs are of a uniform size and shape, if there aren't any oddly shaped or bent twigs that are disturbing the bundle. So it goes from "in unity there is strength" to "in uniformity there is strength," and from there it proceeds to the excesses of fascism as we've seen them exercised throughout the twentieth century and into the twenty-first.

Now anarchy, on the other hand, is almost starting from the principle that "in diversity, there is strength," which makes much more sense from the point of view of looking at the natural world. Nature, and the forces of evolution—if you happen to be living in a country where they still believe in the forces of evolution, of course—did not really see fit to follow that "in unity and in uniformity there is strength" idea. If you want to talk about successful species, then you're talking about bats and beetles; there are thousands of different varieties of bat and beetle. Certain sorts of tree and bush have diversified so splendidly that there are now thousands of examples of this basic species. Now you contrast that to something like horses or humans, where there's one basic type of human, and two maybe three basic types of horses. In terms of the evolutionary tree, we are very bare, denuded branches. The whole program of evolution seems to be to diversify, because in diversity there is strength.

And if you apply that on a social level, then you get something like anarchy. Everybody is recognized as having their own abilities, their own particular agendas, and everybody has their own need to work cooperatively with other people. So it's conceivable that the same kind of circumstances that obtain in a small human grouping, like a family or like a collection of friends, could be made to obtain in a wider human grouping like a civilization.

So I suppose those are pretty much my thoughts at the moment upon anarchy. Although of course with anarchy, it's a fairly shifting commodity, so if you ask me tomorrow I might have a different idea.

Margaret: *In "writing for comics" you write about how stories can have relevance to the world around us, how stories can be "useful" in some way. How do you think that stories can be useful? And how do politics inform your work?*

Alan: Well, I think that stories are probably more than just useful; they are probably vital. I think that if you actually examine the relationship between real life and fiction, you'll find that we most often predicate our real lives upon fictions that we have applied from somewhere. From our earliest days in the caves I'm certain we have, when assembling our own personalities, tried to borrow qualities—perhaps from real people that we admire, but as often as not from some completely mythical person, some god or some hero, some character from a storybook. Whether this is a good idea or not, this tends to be what we do. The way that we talk, the way that we act, the way that we behave, we're probably taking our example from some fiction or prototype. Even if it's a real person who's inspiring us, it may be that *they* were partly inspired by fictional examples. And given that, it is quite easy to see that in a sense, our entire lives—individually or as a culture—are a kind of narrative.

It's a kind of fiction, it is not a reality in the sense that it is something concrete and fixed; we constantly fictionalize our own experience. We edit our own experience. There are bits of it that we simply misremember, and there are bits of it that we deliberately edit out because they're not of interest to us or perhaps they show us in a bad light. So we're constantly revising, both as individuals and as nations, our own past. We're turning it moment by moment into a kind of fiction, that is the way that we assemble our daily reality. We are not experiencing reality directly, we are simply experiencing our perception of reality. All of these signals pulsing down optic nerves, and in the tympanums of our ears, from those we compose, moment by moment, our view of reality. And inevitably, because people's perceptions are different, and the constructions that people put on things are different, then there is no such thing as a cold, objective reality that is solid and fixed and not open to interpretation. Inevitably, we are to some

> Inevitably there is going to be a political element in everything that we do or don't do. In everything we believe, or do not believe.

extent creating a fiction every second of our lives, the fiction of who we are, the fiction of what our lives are about, the meanings that we give to things.

So to some degree, stories are at the absolute center of human existence. Sometimes to disastrous effect; if you think about how various ancient religious stories—that may have been intended at the time as no more than fables—have led to so many devastating wars up to and including the present day. Obviously there are some occasions when the fictions that we base our lives upon lead us into some terrifying territory. So yes, I think that stories have a great part to play, in some ways more than the development of laws or the development of any other kind of sociological marker. I think that it is the development of our fictions and the development of our stories that tend to be the real measure of our progress. I tend to think that when we look back at culture, we're generally looking at art as the measure of the high points of our culture. We're not looking at war, or the major, benign political events. We're generally looking at cultural high points, such as a story.

As to how politics relate to the storytelling process, I'd say that it's probably in the same way that politics relate to everything. I mean, as the old feminist maxim used to go, "the personal is the political." We don't really live in an existence where the different aspects of our society are compartmentalized in the way that they are in bookshops. In a bookshop, you'll have a section that is about history, that is about politics, that is about the contemporary living, or the environment, or modern thinking, modern attitudes. All of these things are political. All of these things are *not* compartmentalized; they're all mixed up together. And I think that inevitably there is going to be a political element in everything that we do or don't do. In everything we believe, or do not believe.

I mean, in terms of politics I think that it's important to remember what the word actually means. Politics sometimes sells itself as having an ethical dimension, as if there was good politics and bad politics. As far as I understand it, the word actually has the same root as the word polite. It is the art of conveying information in a politic way, in a way that will be discrete and diplomatic and will offend the least people. And basically we're talking about spin. Rather than being purely a late twentieth, early twenty-first century term, it's obvious that politics have always been nothing but spin. But, that said, it is the system which is interwoven with our everyday lives, so every aspect our lives is bound to have a political element, including writing fiction.

I suppose any form of art can be said to be propaganda for a state of mind. Inevitably, if you are creating a painting, or writing a story, you are making propaganda, in a sense, for the way that you feel, the way that you think, the way that you see the world. You are trying to express your own view of reality and existence, and that is inevitably going to be a political action—especially if your view of existence is too far removed from the mainstream view of existence. Which is how an awful lot of writers have gotten into terrible trouble in the past.

Margaret: *Have you run into any problems with your publishers, owing to your radical politics?*

Alan: Well, no, surprisingly. I largely got into comics under the influence of the American underground comics; that was probably the background that I was coming from, a kind of adulation of American underground culture, including its comic strips. Now, that background was always very, very political. So right from the start there would probably always be some politically satirical element, at least from time to time.

When it was necessary, or felt right for the story, there would be some satirical political element creeping in to my work right from the earliest days. A lot of the very early little short stories I did for *2000AD*, little twist-ending science-fiction tales. When it was possible I would try to get some kind of political moral, or simply moral, into stories like that. Simply because it made them better stories, and it made me feel better about writing them because I was expressing my own beliefs.

Now because those stories were popular, because they sold more comics, I never had any problem at all. Even if the people publishing the books didn't share my beliefs or politics—and in most instances their politics would have been 180 degrees away from mine—they at least understood their own sales figures. And they seemed to be able to live with that, with publishing views to which they themselves they did not subscribe, so long as the readers were buying the books in large numbers. They are prepared to forgive you anything if you're making enough money for them. I think that's the general message that I've taken from my career in comics: that if you're good enough, if you're popular enough, if you're making enough money, then they will quite cheerfully allow you to use their publishing facilities to disseminate ideas that perhaps are very, very radical. Perhaps even in some contexts, potentially dangerous. This is the beauty of capitalism: there is an inherent greed that is more concerned with raking in the money than in whatever message might be being circulated. So no, I've never really had any problems with that.

Margaret: *Can you point to any effect that your stories have had on the world?*

Alan: I can't think of many *positive* ones. I would like to think that some of my work has opened up people's thinking about certain areas. On a very primitive level, it would be nice to think that people thought a little bit differently about the comics medium as a result of my work, and saw greater possibility in it. And realized what a useful tool for disseminating information it was. That would be an accomplishment. That would have added a very useful implement to the arsenal of people who are seeking social change, because comics can be an incredibly useful tool in that regard. I'd also like to think that perhaps, on a higher level, that some of my work has the potential to radically change enough people's ideas upon a subject. To perhaps, eventually, decades after my own death, affect some kind of minor change in the way that people see and organize society. Some of my magical work that I've done is an attempt to get people to see reality and it's possibilities in a different light. I'd like to think that that might have some kind of impact eventually. I'd like to think that *Lost Girls*, with its attempt to rehabilitate the whole notion of pornography, might have some benign effects. That people will be able to potentially come up with a form of pornography which is not ugly, which is intelligent, and which potentially makes pornography into a kind of beautiful, welcoming arena in which our most closely guarded sexual secrets can be discussed in an open and healthy way. Where our shameful fantasies are not left to fester and to turn into something monstrous in the dark inside us. It would be nice to think that maybe stuff like *Lost Girls* and the magical material might have the potential to actually change the way people think.

With relation to the magic, I can remember one of the last conversations I had with my very dear and much missed friend, the writer Kathy Acker. This was very soon after I had just become interested and involved with magic. I was saying to her how the way I was then seeing things was that basically magic was about the last and best bastion of revolution. The political revolution, the sexual revolution, these things had their part and had their limits, whereas the idea of a magical revolution would revolve around actually changing people's consciousnesses, which is to say, actually changing the nature of perceived reality. Kathy agreed with that completely—it sort of followed on some of her own experiences—and I still think that that is true. In some ways, magic is the most political of all of the areas that I'm involved with.

For example, we were talking earlier—well *I* was talking earlier—about anarchy and fascism being the two poles of politics. On one hand you've got fascism, with the bound bundle of twigs, the idea that in unity and uniformity there is strength; on the other you have anarchy, which is completely determined by the individual, and where the individual determines his or her own life. Now if you move that into the spiritual domain, then in religion, I find very much the spiritual equivalent of fascism. The word "religion" comes from the root word *ligare*, which is the same root word as ligature, and ligament, and basically means "bound together in one belief." It's basically the same as the idea behind fascism; there's not even necessarily a spiritual component it. Everything from the Republican Party to the Girl Guides could be seen as a religion, in that they are bound together in one belief. So to me, like I said, religion becomes very much the spiritual equivalent of fascism. And by the same token, magic becomes the spiritual equivalent of anarchy, in that it is purely about self-determination, with the magician simply a human being writ large, and in more dramatic terms, standing at the center of his or her own universe. Which, I think, is a kind of a spiritual statement of the basic anarchist position. I find an awful lot in common between anarchist politics and the pursuit of magic, that there's a great sympathy there.

> I find religion to be very much the spiritual equivalent of fascism. And by the same token, magic becomes the spiritual equivalent of anarchy.

Margaret: *Have you heard of the A for Anarchy project that happened in New York City with the release of the movie version of* V for Vendetta?

Alan: No I haven't, please go on, inform me.

Margaret: *Some anarchist activist types started tabling outside of the movie showings with information about how Hollywood had taken the politics out of the movie.*

Alan: Ah, now that is fantastic, that is really good to hear, because that's one of the things that had distressed me. What had originally been a straightforward battle of ideas between anarchy and fascism had been turned into a kind of ham-fisted parable of 9-11 and the war against terror, in which the words anarchy and fascism appear nowhere. I mean, at the time I was thinking: look, if they wanted to protest about George Bush and the way that American society is going since 9-11— which would completely understandable—then why don't they do what I did back in the 1980s when I didn't like the way that England was going under Margaret Thatcher, which is to do a story in my own country, that was clearly about events that were happening right then in my own country, and kind of make it obvious that that's what you're talking about. It struck me that for Hollywood to make *V for Vendetta*, it was a way for thwarted and impotent American liberals to feel that they were making some kind of statement about how pissed off they were with the current situation without really risking anything. It's all set in England, which I think that probably, in *most* American eyes, is kind of a fairytale kingdom where we still perhaps have giants. It doesn't really exist; it might as well be in the Land of Oz for most Americans. So you can set your political parable in this fantasy environment called

England, and then you can vent your spleen against George Bush and the neo-conservatives. Those were my feelings, and I must admit those are completely based upon not having seen the film even once, but having read a certain amount of the screenplay. That was enough.

But that's really interesting about the A for Anarchy demonstrations. That's fantastic. Ⓐ

"Everybody is trying to compete to convert people to their ideology. But it seems like the revolutionary thing would be to get people to look at ideologies differently."

—Anonymous CrimethInc. Ex-Worker

A CRIMETHINC. EX-WORKER

CrimethInc. is a collective entity that invites open participation: anyone can write, organize, and publish under the name. For the past decade or so they have turned out an incredible body of books, in many ways revitalizing the world of anarchist publishing. Their books are high quality, available quite cheaply, well-designed, and speak to a different audience than a lot of other anarchist literature. While much of the "history" in Days of War, Nights of Love *might be considered fiction, I was also deeply interested in their two children's books:* The Secret World of Duvbo *and* The Secret World of Terijan. *Since this interview, they've also released* Expect Resistance, *a unique book that moves between fictional narrative and theoretical essay quite fluidly.*

After a brief email correspondence, I had the pleasure of interviewing an anonymous author who, along with many others, writes under the CrimethInc. moniker. We climbed up into a dusty belfry while a radical bookfair bustled beneath our feet. And contrary to the way most interviews go, this one started with the author asking me *a question:*

CrimethInc.: What did you think the main differences between *The Secret World of Terijian* and *The Secret World of Duvbo* were?

Margaret: *Well, they were both trying to get a political point across, but the* Duvbo *book had a lot more subtlety to it; it* *wasn't as much about fighting as it was about discovering your imagination, as compared to the* Terijian *book, which was "kids discover the ELF."*

CrimethInc.: I don't think that they're too different. The *Duvbo* story is supposed to bring out the ways in which the dynamics within people and communities contribute to their subjugation. They're subjugated by their own inertia, their cultural norms, and their fear of acknowledging all the secret parts of themselves. It's an optimistic story; in the end, it is only two ruling class people against the whole town.

Whereas with *Terijian*, it's actually two protagonists versus the world; their parents aren't on board for the struggle. Well, there's the two kids and then there are the ELFs—there are just a few of them.

Perhaps you could argue that both books bring out the limitations or shortcomings of the political programs they propose. I hadn't thought about this until now, but the former book seems to suggest, "We're all anarchists in waiting and if we could just be openly what we secretly are, everything will change. The ruling powers will just leave." It's a little optimistic, like I said. *Terijian*—which is a benefit for the Green Scare victims—tells a story similar to the one that the Green Scare came out of: it's just us, and maybe a few other people, but we'll never know who they are because they're in masks, and we're the ones who have to make a revolution against normal society. That's also not a recipe for success. I mean, the parents don't get involved in the struggle, they're not punching the construction workers in the end, and the construction workers aren't punching their bosses.

Terijian is a true story, in that the authors see it as a sort of allegory of the Minnehaha Freestate. *Duvbo* is like a creation myth for a world that hasn't come to be yet.

Margaret: *What are you attempting to accomplish when you write fiction? Do you think you have accomplished anything with your fiction writing?*

CrimethInc.: There are writers whose whole project is to express themselves: "This really expresses me, these are my innermost feelings." Personally, I'm not interested in that. I think that writing is an attempt to... if I say the word "communicate," it sounds like there is some sort of object that is in one place that I'm attempting to convey to another place, and I would rather use a word that emphasizes that you're trying to create a dynamic between people by introducing some new force, which is the words. So for me, writing isn't about expressing myself, like I have some thing inside of me that I have to bring out and I'll give it to people and they'll be different or richer or something. It's more like it's a way to exert a lever on social situations. So I'm not possessive of my work per se; I try to contribute to the social milieu, or to the ongoing dialogue, in such a way that things happen.

I think non-fiction is overrated in terms of how *non-*fiction it is. Everything that you write is going to be a construct; when you're writing history you're choosing to leave out 99.9% of everything. You're basically making up a story by choosing what to include. You could tell the story of the Spanish civil war by writing about what everyone had for breakfast every morning. The fact that we throw out the breakfasts and focus only on the military engagements or what was mentioned in the newspapers, that's not totally true to reality. But how could you be true to reality?

So writing fiction is just a way to let yourself off the hook: "I'm telling a story." Maybe it's a way to be *more* accountable, because you're actually telling a story and that's the focus, the story, as opposed to, "Oh, this is the truth," which is debatable in every case, be it a historical truth or a philosophical truth.

Margaret: *CrimethInc. is both famous and notorious for blurring history and fiction anyway. In* Days of War, Nights of Love, *there are all the references to fictional historical events or a certain spin on historical events. What led CrimethInc. to do that?*

CrimethInc.: I'm not sure that I can answer for everything in *Days of War.* You can sort of tell that *Days of War* was put together by enthusiastic young people who were saying to themselves, "Fuck it! Let's just say this! Let's see what happens!" That can have bad results or good results. The exciting thing about *Days of War* is the vitality; you can tell that the people who put it together weren't thinking about it as a book that a lot of people were going to read. And that's the kind of fearlessness that you can only have once as a publisher; once everything you put out under that name is going to receive attention, your actions are whole lot heavier. It's a lot harder to move that freely.

> Why do things ourselves? I mean, fuck capitalism, you know?

One of the aspects of free motion in that book is the devil-may-care approach to history: "Oh, we'll just say this, maybe it happened, maybe it didn't." One of the points of that, presumably, is to cast into doubt all the other books that say, "This happened, and this was the truth." *Days of War* seems to proclaim, "Don't believe us, obviously we're making things up; maybe you shouldn't believe them either, maybe they're making things up." Maybe all the other books you can get are also fabrications, constructions, or at least should be treated as such.

One might say the traditional way to approach activism or radical literature is to ask, "How do we get people to believe our new idea? How do we get people to believe this new ideology?" That's not actually particularly useful. Everybody is trying to compete to convert people to their ideology. It seems like the revolutionary thing would be to get people to look at ideologies and reality differently. That would be a part of moving to another phase of revolutionary struggle. So how do you write a book that simultaneously calls itself and all other books into question, in such a way that it has a dynamic effect on the readership rather than persuading people to your opinion? In the regard you mention, *Days of War* is a clumsy but audacious attempt to answer that question.

Margaret: *Why do you choose to be anonymous under the CrimethInc. moniker?*

CrimethInc.: As I mentioned, I'm not convinced by the myth of authorship. "These are my thoughts, I came up with them, they're under my name." That whole copyright thing? That's all about private property. Folk songs—before so-called "riot" folk I mean—there are songs that nobody knows who wrote them, everybody sings them. They're collective property. Everybody adjusts them to their specific situations. I think that that's a much more sensible format. All sorts of CrimethInc. material has been published about the question of authorship, so maybe I'd better focus on my own choices, rather than the ideological ones?

First of all, I want to emphasize that language and all the stories inside of it are collectively produced. That is not to say that they are horizontally produced, but they are collectively produced. Capitalism is collectively produced: it's a collective relation that we all participate in, in some ways, but a hierarchical one. We collectively produce language, we collectively produce our ideas. They come out of the conversations we're all having. One person takes some ideas that have been gestating for hundreds of years, writes a book about them, puts his name on it, and makes a whole lot of money or a whole lot of intellectual capital, wins a whole lot of respect, for being the person who's basically privatized this previously wild rainforest of ideas. I think that's bullshit.

Authorship can be useful for accountability, if you're making a claim that you need to be personally answerable for. But if you're testing out an idea on other people, I think removing the authorship can be a pretty good thing. "Don't worry about me and how exciting my biography is—how does this idea affect you? Does it just bounce off of you? Is it useless to you? Is it exciting?"

I'm interested in seeing language play out as a dynamic between people. Not as an expression of one person's personal reality, but as a collective construction. And personally, in addition to finding that critique compelling, I'm just not interested in being some John Zerzan or Ernest Hemingway or something, who has to contend with more people knowing my shadow self than my real self. I enjoy working collectively on writing projects with other people; I think that I'm more intelligent contributing to a collective process of writing, just as people are generally more articulate in conversation than they are when they have to compose a monologue extemporaneously. I don't think anybody deserves, in the good sense or the bad sense, the positives that Hemingway gets. Nobody deserves the misery of being a famous public figure, upon whom everybody else can project their personal psychodramas and resentments.

Margaret: *I feel like that happens to a certain degree with the moniker CrimethInc.*

CrimethInc.: Well, CrimethInc.'s not important. Everybody can hate CrimethInc. and that's not a problem. It's like a false front to absorb all the projections, all the good and bad associations, so that the people involved in it can still be the real individuals they are in their communities, doing the things they care about, without being crippled by people walking up to them on the street and being like, "Oh my god, it's really you, sign my blah blah blah."

Since a lot of the attitudes around authors tend toward mythologizing, better to present something that is explicitly a myth for people to mythologize and leave the people who are involved with the project free to go about their real lives.

Margaret: *Why did CrimethInc. choose to self-publish?*

CrimethInc.: Self-management. CrimethInc. is just a name that a small group of people initially started sticking on self-published projects, with the critique that it is best to have control of what you're doing. This is a long-running question that goes back much further than The Clash signing with a major label. Let's say you're trying to get to know people in your town. Do you go to their parties or throw your own parties? If you only throw your own parties, maybe you'll only meet the people you can persuade to come to them, but you can create an environment that brings what you want out of those interactions—what's good for you, and hopefully will be good for the people who choose to come. If you only go to other people's parties, you'll

One person takes all the ideas that have been gestating for hundreds of years, writes a book about them, puts his name on them, and makes a whole lot of money or a whole lot of intellectual capital, a whole lot of respect, for being the person who's basically privatized this previously wild rainforest of ideas. I think that's bullshit.

always have a limited agency in framing the interactions you have with others.

I remember when they killed Brad Will in Oaxaca, a year ago now, it was right before Halloween. We went to someone's Halloween party to try to turn people out to come occupy the Mexican consulate with us. We were trying to explain to people that our friend had just been killed, at some fucking party where everybody was just there to drink. It's sort of a stretch, as metaphors go, but that is why we have our own dinner parties, right, so we can have a space in which the dialogue is about the things that are important to us. I was at some else's fancy vegan bourgeois Halloween party where everyone's in costumes and they don't give a fuck about my friend who got killed, you know what I'm saying? They care about me, but it's not a space in which we can discuss that, let alone discuss what to do.

> Someone might publish an amazing anarchist text that lots of people would then read, but the question isn't how to get everyone to read anarchist texts, the question is how we can interact in anarchic ways.

So first of all, we're creating a space that is self-organized and controlled by everyone who participates in it. CrimethInc. isn't necessarily the most radical experiment in this direction, but it's significant that the name itself, if not all of the structures that exist under it, is open and freely accessible to all. The *Terijian* book was published by a totally different group of people than the people who are involved in crimethinc.com. That particular website is still an exclusive and difficult-to-participate-in structure, but the CrimethInc. myth itself is open and accessible to the public.

Why do things ourselves? I mean, fuck capitalism, you know? The initial projects that I was aware of were ones in which people were committing small-scale crime, taking the money, and making free things out of it, saying, "Here's some free things funded by anti-capitalist crime—can we have some more of this please?" When you first got a copy of *Evasion* in zine form, and you're reading the zine, you're some 16-year-old kid, it dawns on you that obviously, that zine was stolen and is a sign of an entire underground community of people who believe in anti-corporate theft as a ethical way of life. The zine is the message, however repetitive and dumb the text in it may be.

I think the content of self-organization is worth 1,000 times whatever you can say. I'm sure Verso [largest English language radical book publisher] or someone might publish an amazing anarchist text that lots of people would then read, but the question isn't how to get everyone to read anarchist texts, the question is how we can interact in anarchic ways. You can assign Bakunin at Columbia University and the world won't be any more anarchist.

Margaret: *[Here, dear reader, I rambled incoherently for a moment before reaching my point.] I know that CrimethInc. in particular is a scapegoat for people's accusations of lifestylism.*

CrimethInc.: You're talking about The Wooden Shoe [a Philadelphia anarchist bookstore] not carrying *Evasion*? I support The Wooden Shoe's choice to not carry *Evasion*. [Note: *Evasion* is a zine that CrimethInc. published in book form, a memoir of a traveling shoplifter that offended some people through its flippant view on homelessness and lack of class critique.] *Evasion* wasn't made to be sold at The Wooden Shoe in its book form. The people who are going to The Wooden Shoe need other things that are available at The Wooden Shoe much more than they need *Evasion*. *Evasion* was made, specifically in book form at least, to subvert the materialism of a certain class of youth, by valorizing another mode of life, not as an end in itself, but with the understanding that if those alternate values were presented as a possibility, as an exciting possibility, that they could only lead, at least for some people, to readers eventually developing a deeper anti-capitalist analysis. I feel that that book has served that purpose in some circles. That's the great thing about us organizing horizontally—freedom of association is one of the other anarchist catchphrases: if people don't want to organize with us it's fine. It's not like the CrimethInc. distribution hub is some giant monolith that if you don't take all of the books suddenly you can't get any of the other books you want either. That what's good about things being structured on a more horizontal basis: everybody can take care of their own stuff rather than depending on one big distributor.

Back to what I said about The Clash signing to that big record label, as one of the first punk bands to sell out or whatever: if all of the energy that had been put into that compromise had been put into building autonomous structures instead, it would be so much easier for us to circulate our ideas today without reinforcing hierarchies. I think that it's absolutely worth whatever you won't be able to do, whatever the drawbacks of doing things yourself are, to reinforce the culture of self-directed activity.

We did finally have to work with Ingram, the giant distributor, to get books into the libraries. I grew up reading books in the library. I think that that is important, that's one of the few currently existing communal forms of wealth, our libraries. The way I understand the way the distribution is set up, first the books go into all the DIY channels of circulation that are available, then they also go to Ingram and the bigger distributors, so that people who can't find them in the DIY environment maybe encounter them elsewhere, because it's also not good to keep our projects a secret. Ingram and all of those motherfuckers... you know, to get one ISBN number you have to buy 10 of them, so you can't just be one person with a book. I think we need more cooperatives, more groups of people who would need ten ISBN numbers, so the individuals don't get screwed. I'm not saying that that is a solution to capitalism, but it *is* a way to collectively organize in the meantime. Ⓐ

"We should be trading
our books for change...
not pocket change. If you
want my book, plant some
tomatoes in the boulevard or
burn an SUV."

—Professor Calamity

PROFESSOR CALAMITY
of the Catastraphone Orchestra

Professor Calamity is a writer who collaborates with his mechanical band The Catastraphone Orchestra to write steampunk fiction & theory and with The Curious George Brigade to write anarchist theory. The former are perhaps best known for their fictional seasonals that appear in SteamPunk Magazine, *the latter for their excellent non-fiction book* Anarchy in the Age of Dinosaurs. *As one of his two editors for* SteamPunk Magazine, *it wasn't particularly hard to track him down, but his opinions on the subject matter at hand were quite invigorating.*

Margaret: *How did you first come into fiction writing?*

Calamity: I think I've always written fiction, since I was a child. I was always interested in telling my own stories; I started by telling stories about the movies I saw in posters. I remember clearly, when I was about six, my father was out on a prolonged strike and we were very poor. We were receiving government cheese, bags of powdered milk, and a sack of groceries from the union HQ every week. My brother and I had always loved movies and would go every Saturday to a run-down theater (an old opera house actually) that showed hammer films and other "cheapies" on weekend matinées and seventies pornos in the evenings. While my father was on strike we couldn't go to the movies obviously, so I would make up stories for my brother and our friends (their parents were on strike also). I wrote a few of them down and a next-door neighbor drew some pictures to go along with it.

I guess I always found the writing experience to be collaborative, despite the myth of the lonely writer and the typewriter. In school I loved writing fiction because it was a chance to escape from the confines of rural Wisconsin and explore places and ideas that were alien to the conservative community I grew up in. I never wrote for myself (another writer myth I never bought into); I was always writing for my friends, stories I liked but also things that they might enjoy. Sometimes three or four of us would get together after high school and smoke stolen cigarettes, drink warm beer, and write for hours on various projects. We would take each other's characters, ideas, and whatnot and just write with and about them. It gave us a sense of freedom. It wasn't about ego, capital-A art, exorcising personal demons, or any of that jazz. It was just fun to see where we could take ideas and characters. In college I took some creative writing classes but hated it. I hated the egos and the pretentiousness. I wanted to tell stories and share ideas, not compete to see who was the most clever or well-read. After graduate school, I took my still-wet anthropology degree and went to Bulgaria to live in a Roma (gypsy) ghetto. I went with a bunch of other young writers, and as Bulgaria was lurching from totalitarian communism to totalitarian capitalism, we drank plum brandy and wrote plays. There was a sort of craziness during that period, but it was very productive and was probably the period during which I spent the most time writing fiction. Now I have less time.

Margaret: *What about politics? How did you first get interested in anarchism?*

Calamity: In high school I was a Marxist. I wore a black boiler suit every day with a hammer & sickle pin in my wool cap and

I had a smug-looking Marx hanging in my locker. Needless to say, I was the only Marxist in my small school. It wasn't until I met other communists in college that I saw how fuckin' authoritarian they were. I found some books by Emma Goldman and Hakim Bey and started getting into the idea of anarchy. I met the Church of Anarchy folks in Madison, Wisconsin and did some political work with them. We started a small collective called "Some Madison Anarchists." That was 19 years ago, and the funny thing is we are all still anarchists, working in different parts of the country, doing political projects.

Margaret: *How do you think that being an anarchist affects your writing style? You say that you write collectively. Can you talk a bit about that?*

Calamity: I only write using a collective approach. This takes many different forms, depending on the individuals I am working with. I write non-fiction with the Curious George Brigade and we do it by arguing about every line and having long discussions about every topic before we start hitting the keyboard. When I write fiction, we usually talk first about the ideas and characters. We verbally hash out the story and then huddle around the computer and take turns typing. Someone not from the group then usually reads it and does minor edits and then we get together and talk about it in some detail. The writing group may go back and re-write bits of it. Sometimes I will write whole chapters and then a group will meet to discuss it and offer major edits and changes. Someone else will rewrite the entire chapter and then it gets "filtered" again. It's a consensus process and you have to have pretty thick skin to go through it. You have to give up ownership and see it as a real collaboration. It's funny—in many ways the collaborative process can be as creative as the actual wordsmithing and writing. I hate editing, but in a group it's a less grating process. Others despise doing dialog and so on; we try to compliment each other. You have to be able to laugh to make it work, even when you're writing serious or tragic stuff.

Margaret: *How about vice-versa? Do you think your love of fiction affects your politics at all?*

Calamity: I don't trust political people who don't appreciate fiction. Too much of our politics, even anarchist politics, lacks imagination. The problems are so numbing in their complexity and scope that we *need* to be able to draw upon the most imaginative solutions possible to have any chance. I also believe that fiction tends to be more effective propaganda for the extreme left than Noam Chomsky-esque critiques. So much of the far left political writing lacks a heart; it's so cerebral now. I feel like the anarchists of the past had more heart than many of my comrades today. Anarchists may be smarter than they were in the past, but they miss the human connections that can make our isolated scene a real movement.

I know we're all hypocrites but I'm not sure we should be so unashamed about it. So much of our hypocrisy seems to be simply a reflection of our lack of creativity rather than the result of some deep-seated, inescapable paradox.

Margaret: *It comes up a lot, that at any given point protests or anarchism or whatever are stagnant, lack imagination... I suppose that fiction is a good venue to explore possibilities. But maybe it's more than that, or maybe it's just a way for individuals to develop their own creativity?*

Calamity: Fiction has had and will continue to have an important role to play in radical politics. One can look at *Uncle Tom's Cabin*, *The Grapes of Wrath* [editor's note: this book first turned me on to politics], *The Jungle*, *The Monkeywrench*

Gang, and the works of Dickens. That's just a short list of how fiction can impact real politics. Fiction can speak to the heart, something that's much needed for anarchist struggles. We're talking about a radical change, not just in economic terms but also in how we relate to each other and the world. I would think fiction would be better at articulating this than non-fiction. It is not surprising to me that totalitarian regimes like the Nazis, Italian Fascists, Bolsheviks, etc. first ban (and then burn) fiction works as dangerous. Fiction has a strange power to move people and "stick" with them.

Margaret: *What, if anything, do you hope to accomplish through writing, particularly fictional stories?*

Calamity: I hope to accomplish the liberation of my brothers and sisters and the utter destruction of authority. Failing that, I hope to tell a darn good story that isn't too tidy. I like ambiguity; not the clever post-modern obscurantism, but the messy everyday ambiguity we all experience. My stuff is too dark probably to be considered inspiring, though. Someday I'd like to inspire, but it would have to be honest.

Margaret: *I suppose your work does have a fairly dark tone, often very fatalistic or nihilistic. Do you think that mirrors how you see the political situation? Or is it a reflection of something else?*

Calamity: I think the world we live in is pretty bleak (though I am pretty upbeat in person). I've always been attracted to characters living in very bleak times, how they're shaped by those times yet still resist. To me the history of resistance isn't overly heroic or something to wish for, but a necessity. A necessity that can be quite dark. I guess I'm just very skeptical of Pollyanna-ish heroism. If it were easy it wouldn't be called "struggle." The fact is that many in the resistance will become lost, their lives will not be great adventures and no one will write folk songs about them, yet they continue. That's what interests me. I think of Winston in *1984*, who is a nobody and ends tragically, but is real and is someone we can identify with. I feel fiction should present some human truths and the truth is that most of us will *not* succeed even if we are smart and struggle hard, but that doesn't diminish our cause. In a sense, it's optimistic to think that people will stand up and fight back even when they are going to lose. That's something that is lost in most American fiction.

Margaret: *You've helped organize the NYC anarchist bookfairs. What are your feelings about these events? What do you hope see come out of them?*

Calamity: Again, I am shocked by the lack of imagination at these events. It's like nearly any other subculture trade show. I go because I like the people and out of some warped sense of duty to support any anarchist project, but I just can't see paying for a table to sell goods about overthrowing capitalism. Yeah, I know we're all hypocrites but I'm not sure we should be so unashamed about it. So much of our hypocrisy seems to be simply a reflection of our lack of creativity rather than the result of some deep-seated, inescapable paradox.

Margaret: *What do you think can be done to reinvent the radical bookfair model?*

Calamity: Everything is possible. We could have fictional potlatches. We could hide books in the children's sections of libraries. We could have around-the-clock readings by authors on soapboxes. The money we spend on renting a hall could be spent on a renting a copy machine and people could scam paper and just copy what they want. What about trade for books? What if people stenciled a favorite line or title across the city in exchange for the book they wanted? In fact, what if that was the only way you could get the book? Bookfairs unfortunately achieve an interesting paradox of making books both too expensive and devaluing them. Because of the lack of money in our scenes, the books are often too expensive to take a chance on buying something you wouldn't normally. This leads to an unconscious ghettoization of our reading, since we're only reading things we think we'll enjoy. We're just rereading the same authors, publishers, and whatnot. That's why I like magazines, because there's a hodgepodge of stuff and people actually read stuff they might not ever pick up off a table or plop twelve bucks down for. So bookfairs make books expensive (not any cheaper than buying them online or at a store) and thus we move from a culture of abundance to one of parochial scarcity, yet at the same time they reduce the actual value of the ideas. Most radical authors I know say they write not for money, but to create change. If that's true, then we should be trading our books for change... not pocket change. If you want my book, plant some tomatoes in the boulevard or burn an SUV. That would be of real value to me, not some bullshit royalty. I am sure there are a million other things that could be done to change how we relate to distributing books and writings. Ⓐ

"Just like punk rock—never put authors on pedestals."

—Jimmy T. Hand

JIMMY T. HAND

Jimmy T. Hand isn't well-known. He's an activist who writes fiction and non-fiction that I help publish in zine form with my zine publishing collective Strangers In A Tangled Wilderness. We've published In the Hall of the Mountain King *and* The Road to Either Or, *two autobiographical novellas, as well as a few zines of short stories, including* The Seduction of the Wind, As the Day is Long, The World Below, *and* Here Comes the Fucking Circus. *I spoke to him about the role of storytellers in anarchist culture.*

Margaret: *What are your thoughts about the intersection of fiction and anarchism?*

Jimmy: Oh hell, what a question. Start with something else. Let's come back to that one.

Margaret: *When I interviewed a representative of CrimethInc., they mentioned that they felt that fiction bore a certain amount of honesty, in that "non-fiction" isn't always as non-fictional as people might claim.*

Jimmy: I like that. It's something I've written about myself, in *The Road to Either Or*; people can claim that things are actually history, but are they? The example I used was quoting people. Those quotes are from my memory, and of course, my memory is flawed. I see things through my own lens.

One thing I've been thinking about recently is fiction and... not really anarchism, but about living your life fully. I've been thinking about how stories need conflict to keep the reader interested. I used to be really against that. It just seemed so fabricated, to have every story rotate around some kind of "plot." But then I started thinking about my own life... I became significantly more interested in my own life once I acquired a nemesis: the state. I still read fantasy books, sci-fi books, but I don't do it with the same sense of *longing* that I used to. Do you know what I mean? I used to read books like the *MYTH Inc.* series [by Robert Asprin], or even *Lord of the Rings* [by J.R.R. Tolkien]. Or the *Borderlands* books by Will Shetterly. I used to read those books and I felt like I would give anything to live that way, to have some kind of motivation, to live in a time of fantasy and mystique. But then, when I ran away from home, I discovered that fantastic world, and it was the real world.

Margaret: *What are your thoughts on self-publishing?*

Jimmy: I don't have time to self-publish. [*Laughs*] I'm glad that you take care of all that crap.

Margaret: *I mean about DIY publishing instead of mainstream publishing.*

Jimmy: Yeah. I mean, I guess I can't really fault people either way. Well, maybe it depends on what the book is about. Would I sell my fantasy stories to a mainstream publisher? Probably not. Would I sell my autobiographical stories to a mainstream publisher? Fuck that. With the fiction, it's a different thing, because it's not me telling someone else's story for money. I can understand how authors want to make a living off of what they do; I'm tempted from time to time. But what kind of bastard would I be if I wrote about my story, which is completely inseparable from the stories of my friends and my lover, and then sold it?

I think that all that fantasizing about escape I did when I was younger was probably good for me. Because I recognized it when I found it. It felt the same way, you know? Being washed over in magic. Only this time it was unmediated, because it was me, hopping freight trains, organizing, falling in love every other week. I guess I've calmed down some since then, but it's still there, that feeling. Reading those books was probably good for me. So I guess I could see the case for our *fictional* scenarios and ideas to filter out to the mainstream.

> I used to read books and I feel like I would give anything to live that way, to have some kind of motivation, to live in a time of fantasy and mystique. But then, when I ran away from home, I discovered that fantastic world, and it was the real world.

But if the *real* magic, the *real* scenarios filtered out to the mainstream, it would kill them. Because instead of people learning and discovering things on their own, or through their friends, or the shadowy affiliations of the zine world, they would just recreate exactly what they've read, and we'd have a homogenous culture. Even if that homogenous culture was "anarchist," it really wouldn't be. Besides which, the scenarios *I* fantasize about don't involve mainstream publishing houses existing at all. So wouldn't a story about a fantastic real life be undermined by its own distribution method?

Margaret: *Why do you write fiction? Is there something you hope to accomplish by writing fiction? Can you point to anything you've accomplished?*

Jimmy: Why do I write fiction? I write fiction because I've always wanted to write fiction. Well, and I have all of these ideas floating in my head, of other planets and magical worlds and simple tragic tales—and everything, really—and I really want to express them. I can't draw, I don't have enough friends (or time) to make movies or plays, so I write them down. I like telling stories aloud too. I guess that kind of gets to your second question... what I want to accomplish?

I have this concept in my head of a world where storytellers, or bards or whatever, wander around and tell bedside stories and fireside stories to people, and recreate a kind of folklore. I mean, I guess anarchist culture does it already, but it seems like it's always shoplifting stories or trainhopping stories, or occasionally, and these are more fun, war stories of our resistance. But then, most of *those* stories shouldn't be told, because if no one has been caught for a crime, no one should admit to doing it. And besides, I like stories about hobgoblins who climb trees looking for their lost siblings, wandering through forests filled with unintelligible tourists. You know, *fiction*. So I want to see that culture exist, and the only way I know how to is to just... do it.

Can I point to anything I've accomplished? Honestly? No. Maybe someone, somewhere, has read my stories and thought differently about something, and that would be nice, but if they have, they haven't told me about it yet. And that's alright; it's not about my ego. I mean, creation should be just that: creation. You make something, you give it to the world, and maybe it comes back to you somehow and maybe it doesn't.

So, the intersection of anarchism and fiction. I guess it goes both ways: what are anarchist approaches to fiction? First of all, just like punk rock: never put authors on pedestals. Most of us writers are pretty anti-social, and it's almost like writing and fiction are the only ways we can participate in the anarchist debate. Also, for me, it's like... don't just be an author. It's not enough. In the gift-economy anarchist society I'd like to live in, it wouldn't really be enough to say, "Well, I write books" or, "Well, I tell stories at night in the dance hall." So? Do you grow food? Organize recycling? Dig up concrete? Fight against capitalism? It's like, lots of people play music. That's one thing that is awesome about our scene: most people play music. So at night when our work is done, we all play music together, or maybe we take turns, but there aren't stars. Storytelling should be the same way.

As for the other way around, what fictional, or I guess fantastical, approaches to anarchy could be... I like to think that for one thing, fiction is a good way to work through various scenarios without losing the reader's—or writer's—interest. I hate reading theory, and I know I'm not alone in that. But I love learning about the history of anarchism, or how it could be practiced in the future. Fiction is great for that. And not just real concrete stuff, like anarchy, but for metaphorically exploring so much of the human—or non-human—condition.

And also, a lot of anarchists aren't as social as others. Sometimes we're kinda ostracized. We don't always go to the parties. Sometimes we're more intimidated by the crowds at protest marches than we are by the cops. This doesn't even necessarily make us individualists or not, it just means we need to spend more time alone than a lot of people. So that's what books are for. While you all are dancing and playing music and singing together, maybe I'm in my room or tent or tree or something reading. But just like it's best to relax to music by your friends and comrades, it's best to read escapist work by people who you feel are your peers. Ⓐ

"For me, anarchy is the defiant gesture in the face of overwhelming authority, in defense of the compassionate human spirit. And we need that now more than we ever have."

—Lewis Shiner

LEWIS SHINER

Lewis Shiner writes books that don't sell. They're published by reputable presses. They're finalists and winners of awards. They're earnest and lovely. He is often considered one of the pioneers of cyberpunk. And yet, none of his six novels are in print. In some ways, he's a case study in how a hard-working, capable, dedicated writer can't necessarily make a living at the trade.

For the anarchist, perhaps his most interesting work is Slam, *a novelization of Bob Black's famous essay "The Abolition of Work." He's put much of his work, including his newest novel,* Black & White, *online for free download from his Fiction Liberation Front website:* WWW.FICTIONLIBERATIONFRONT.NET.

I got a chance to read some of his work—most of it can still be found—and talk to him about anarchy, genre fiction, the Wobblies, and why you should be a patron of your own art.

Margaret: *So the main idea that I'm talking to authors about is the intersection between anarchism and fiction, about what kind of role fiction takes in anarchist struggle, and about what kind of influence anarchist ideas have on our fiction.*

Lewis: In thinking about how to answer this, the first place I get stuck is figuring out What Anarchy Means to Me. I mean, we all can sort of point to some of the same things—the WTO demonstrations in Seattle, skaters in circle-A T-shirts, the Sex Pistols—and say "that's anarchy." But what do we really mean by that?

The dictionary definition talks about lawlessness and the absence of governmental authority—but in all seriousness, that's what happening to the entire world right now as corporations rape and pillage the planet, committing one heinous crime after another with no accountability, and government stands by and holds their coats. Clearly that's not what we're talking about. Defiance of authority in the name of individual freedom could describe the nutcases in the Libertarian Party who say that the solution to violence is to arm everybody, and the good guys will just gun the bad guys down as soon as they start any trouble. I hope that's not what we're talking about either.

So I guess for me anarchy is the defiant gesture in the face of overwhelming authority, in defense of the compassionate human spirit. And we need that now more than we ever have. You can't change things through politics—the political process just ratifies the reigning ideas of the culture. Right now our culture is dominated by hate and greed and fear. Even the so-called "progressive" candidates are terrified of being seen as "soft" on terror. In order to get meaningful political change, you have change the culture. Art is one of the few things that can do that. The more that art can show positive images of defiance and rebellion against our culture of greed, the more chance we stand of making changes in the real world.

Margaret: *One thing that others have brought up is that sometimes fiction is a good way to get across theoretical ideas without resorting to theory. It seems like your novel* Slam *does that. On one level, it was kind of like Bob Black's essay "The Abolition of Work," in novel form...*

Lewis: I absolutely and consciously wanted to set up a laboratory where I could turn Black's ideas loose and see how they would play out in that artificial world. There was a very interesting novel called *The End of Mr. Y* by Scarlett Thomas that deals with thought experiments and, by implication, the idea that the novel itself is a thought experiment. My goal in my writing, at least at the moment, is to subvert the capitalist mindset. Any and all ideas about how to do that, and what comes after, are extremely welcome. Anarchists are among the few people actively pursuing that.

Margaret: *What are your associations with anarchism?*

Lewis: Well, as I said when we first discussed doing this interview, I don't hold much claim to being an anarchist myself. I have a day job. I own a lot of stuff (mostly books). I don't hide my political opinions, but I'm not in the street protesting either—well, not lately, anyway. It's a question of where I think I can do the most good. And I believe that using my writing for culture change is the most effective thing I can do toward bringing down the system. And as I said above, I look to anarchists for inspiration, for those gestures of defiance that I can use in my work.

Margaret: *For me, at least, anarchism and/or "being an anarchist" is a matter of self-identification. If you believe that humans would be better off organized horizontally than hierarchically, you're an anarchist (or an autonomist, or whatever). Of course, I know plenty of people, anarchist and otherwise, who would take issue with that definition. But I certainly don't think the protest movement (which I suppose I would say that I'm a part of) has any particular reason to claim that it holds the secret of how to become an anarchist. It has a lot more to do with how we treat each other on a personal level, anyhow.*

You can't change things through politics—the political process just ratifies the reigning ideas of the culture.

Lewis: It's funny—in thinking about this, I finally decided that I'm just reluctant to identify myself with any group or label, whether it's cyberpunk or science fiction writer or anarchist. Maybe that's the surest sign that I *am* an anarchist. I like the idea of horizontal rather than hierarchical arrangements, and I've certainly always had problems with authority in whatever guise, whether it was parents, teachers, bosses, cops, or elected officials.

Margaret: *Speaking of cyberpunk, in the eighties you saw a literary movement you accidentally helped found turn into a cliché, a commodity. What do you think that you had hoped for out of cyberpunk? Do you think its descent into formulaic writing was inevitable?*

Lewis: I never really hoped for anything from cyberpunk. I was very grateful for the publicity, but I never really fit in. I wrote one novel, *Frontera*, that fit the mold, and I certainly enjoyed a lot of the work that people like Gibson and Sterling and Rucker and Shirley were doing. But after that I was off to other stuff.

Cyberpunk, like magical realism, had the misfortune of being easy to imitate. Mirrorshades and implant wetware in the one, butterflies and ghosts in the other.

And yeah, I think it's inevitable that if a certain perceived movement becomes successful, it's going to get commodified and people are going to try to jump on the bandwagon. And cyberpunk, like magical realism, had the misfortune of being easy to imitate. Mirrorshades and implant wetware in the one, butterflies and ghosts in the other.

Margaret: *See, this is frightening to me because I work on* SteamPunk Magazine *and identify with steampunk on aesthetic, political, and social levels. The biggest problem with* that *has become... yeah... airships and brass goggles. Mainstream culture is picking up on the most surface level elements and has run with them. Hell, the same thing happened to punk and its anarchism: suddenly, punk was just about the middle finger, about spray-painted circle-A's. I even* like *airships and tophats and spraypaint and saying "fuck you" to authority, but somehow the mainstream world always picks up on the least threatening elements of this or that culture.*

Lewis: Well, that's society's job, isn't it? To defuse the real threat, on the one hand, and inflate the fake threat on the other? To turn the Black Power movement of the sixties into a cartoon of Afros and raised fists at the same time that it continues to propagate the useful (to bigots) myth that society has to protect white women from black men? To keep pushing the stereotype of the stoned hippie in bell-bottoms and peace symbol at the same time that it terrifies parents that their kids might try marijuana? Michael Moore's *Bowling For Columbine* showed how clearly the current power structure uses fear to manipulate people—and sell them a lot of useless crap. The medical-pharmaceutical-insurance complex is probably the worst, with the military not far behind. Where would Bush have been without 9/11? If there had been no 9/11 he would have had to invent one.

Margaret: *You've mentioned that you're a dues-paying member of the IWW [Industrial Workers of the World—a radical labor union]. How did you first get involved in the Wobblies?*

Lewis: I was a huge fan of Steinbeck in high school, and I loved *The Grapes of Wrath* (and *In Dubious Battle* before that)—speaking of the intersection between anarchism and fiction. So that was where I first heard of the Wobblies. What got me to sign on was a 2005 book called *Wobblies!*, which was a kind of cartoon history of the union. I hadn't even realized they were still around. It was a very effective piece of propaganda, and played into a lot of my existing prejudices—I always knew there was something wrong with the AFL-CIO, for example. The idea of one big union made total sense to me, so I realized I needed to walk it like I talked it.

Margaret: *What has it been like working with mainstream publishers? One of the criticisms you seemed to get a lot for your comic* The Hacker Files, *published by DC comics, was that people disagreed with the political thoughts of the radical protagonist. I have to say, I was hooked by the third page, when Jack Marshall [the protagonist] wore his circle-A shirt to work at the Pentagon.*

Lewis: *The Hacker Files* had a lot of disappointments. For one thing, I love Tom Sutton's art, and I grew to love the man himself in working with him, but he was never a fan favorite. That meant the book was struggling from the outset. I don't like costumed superheroes, and I was forced to use them to try to help sales—but I couldn't help making fun of them, which annoyed the audience I was supposed to be attracting. I can't say how much Marshall's radicalism hurt sales, but to me that was absolutely the heart of the book, so there was never a question about backing down on that. My editor was totally supportive of the political stance of the series, and he was only concerned, as I was, about trying to get it to as many readers as possible.

I like working in comics, but I don't honestly feel like I've done my best work there. I seem to think more in terms of novels than I do visual media like comics or film.

All my novels before the current one were published by mainstream publishers, but that had no effect on the content.

I never made any changes that I didn't agree with, and I never sold any of my books until I was at least well into the second draft. The reason I'm not with a mainstream publisher right now is economics, plain and simple. My books have never sold well, and after five commercial failures, they all gave up on me. Fortunately the guy who runs Subterranean Press, a good-sized independent publisher, is a big fan of my work, and he is willing to give me a home.

Margaret: *Right now it's in the news that DC Comics is suing a charity auction... some comicbook artists got together to sell their art for cancer patients, and DC is suing them for selling drawings of the characters they own. At least with mainsteam-published novels, you still own your characters and work, right?*

Lewis: Sure, I own the characters from my novels and stories—unless I sell them to the movies or TV. And DC and Marvel, at least when I was working for them, were fine with creator-owned projects. The problem is, if you don't sell to the movies you don't make any money. If you play in your own comics sandbox and not the continuity sandbox, you also limit your chance to make a living at it.

This brings up an important point, I think, which is the difficulty of making a living as an artist these days. I think it's harder than it's ever been in history. Part of it is what I call the blockbuster effect. It's the idea that rather than make 100 movies for a million dollars each that would appeal to a wide range of audiences, Hollywood would rather make one movie for 100 million that tries to please everybody. But in doing so they no longer serve people who want intellectual fare or people who don't want to see every problem solved through extreme violence. This same attitude has spread to comics and book publishing as well.

The other piece of the puzzle is the Internet, which has given people the idea that all art should be free. I can understand that people want to cut out the parasitic corporations that make ridiculous profits on art, but at the same time they're guaranteeing that artists don't get paid either. It seems to be okay for artists to give away their work, even though nobody is giving away food or shelter or medical care. So how is that fair?

I did it anyway—I started Fiction Liberation Front, (www. FICTIONLIBERATIONFRONT.NET) where I'm slowly putting all my work on the internet for free download. But I do wonder how this is going to come back to me in terms of anything more than good will. I've talked to some entrepreneur types who are supposed to have answers, but for them it always comes back to sponsorship. So in order for an artist to make a living, you have to hustle up a sponsor. But that doesn't work for me. Even if the sponsor put no strings at all on my content, I am still not going shill for somebody selling SUVs or pharmaceuticals or dead cows. So I have a day job so I can sponsor myself.

Margaret: *Your novel* Slam *immediately gripped me and I read through it in one long session, something I haven't done much since I was a kid. You're clearly a competent writer. What do you think led to your commercial failure? Pure bad luck? Your away-from-center politics?*

Lewis: Well, first off, I'm glad you liked the book. I don't think it's the politics explicitly. It may hurt me that ever since my first novel I have refused to solve the conflicts in my novels through violence (other than violence against property, as in *Slam*). It may hurt me that I don't seem to be able to do the same thing twice. My novels are all in different categories—though it seems to me that if you like one of them, you'll probably like the others.

The only thing I can do is continue to write the sort of novels I want to read, and do the best work I can. Eventually something may click with a wider audience. If not, I'll still have a body of work that I'm proud of. Ⓐ

"If nobody saw the political context behind my stories, I'd probably just get bored. You don't just want to be an entertainer the rest of your life."

—Cristy C. Road

CRISTY C. ROAD

One of the most iconic punk illustrators working today, Cristy C. Road's signature style has graced the cover of many a DIY book and zine. She's been writing and illustrating her own zines for ten years, but she's has stepped into the world of bound books recently as well. Her illustrated novel Bad Habits *blurs the lines of fiction and autobiography just as it blurs the borders of what is, or isn't, a novel.*

She came to do a reading in Baltimore and I met up with her beforehand to talk about what it means for a DIY punk to find commercial success, about learning to connect with people, about working with editors, about what we choose to glorify. And Green Day. We talked about Green Day a lot.

Margaret: *One of the things I wanted to talk to you about is actually something from the acknowledgements in the back of your novel* Bad Habits, *about how a friend told you that changing doesn't mean selling out...*

Cristy: I thanked my friend Holly for letting me know that changing doesn't mean selling out. She's my literary agent. She's this radical woman who grew up with zines, she's a lesbian, and has had all of these experiences that are really inspiring and radical, but you know, she's way older than me and she's a literary agent. She made me realize that I can say what I need to say, make my art, outside of the specifically anarchist community and not compromise what I need to say.

I wanted to make my work accessible to people who aren't me: other Latino people, other queer people, other women who don't have the radical community that supports the way that they think. I just wanted my work out there and accessible to people who have had similar experiences as me but don't have that community to fall back on.

And she made me realize that selling out is more about compromising what you have to say. Like if someone had said, "We'll give you $20,000 if you take this part out of the book," then I would have been like, "Well I don't need your fucking money." But it's been awesome; I did get money for the book. My publisher Soft Skull is rad; they put out so much amazing work. They just put out *Reproduce and Revolt*, which is a collection of radical propaganda put together by the Justseeds collective. They put out a lot of really rad publications and it's awesome that I ended up working with them and not some huge press I wasn't really ready for. But I would've, cause when you're broke you're broke. If someone was like, "Sure, we'll give you 50 grand for your book," I'd say, "And you're not going to make me change the part about this or the part about this?" If they're like, "Yeah," I'll be like, "Fuck yeah, gimme that money." I've been so broke for so long. You've gotta survive. So yeah, change can mean growth. Change doesn't have to mean selling out if you're not compromising your beliefs and what you want to say.

> I can make my art outside of the specifically anarchist community and not compromise what I need to say.

Margaret: *I agree with that. I think it's really important to learn how to speak to groups outside of the niche that we're used to...*

Cristy: To bring them into the niche. [*Laughs*]

Margaret: *That's right. To make multiple niches, so there's not one homogenous radical culture...*

Cristy: But instead a lot of different ones. People are coming from a lot of different backgrounds. Like me, someone who is still in the punk rock scene—have been my whole life—I've never really listened to hip-hop music before. Growing up in Miami, I saw all these hip-hop communities that had the same ideas and wanted to express the same values, but there were things about those communities that I didn't identify with just like there were things about my community that those other people didn't identify with.

It's all about finding ways to cross over, finding things that make us all connect. I'm writing about being queer, about being Latina, about being a woman, and there're a lot of queer Latin girls who aren't punk rock, or a lot of Latin girls who aren't queer, a lot of queer girls who aren't Latin. It's all about finding different things that you can connect with people through.

Margaret: *I was going to ask how you got into writing, if it was through zines and the punk scene...*

Cristy: I started writing my zine [*Greenzine*]—it was all about Green Day—when I was 14. It was very, "I have no friends, I have no community. All I know is Green Day, Lookout! Records, and all the bands affiliated with Green Day." I just wrote this zine about how I can't experience punk rock the way that older people experienced it because I was introduced to it through Green Day, this "sellout" band. But as this gigantic Green Day freak, I knew that they grew up hella poor. And now people have grown; no one is like, "Oh fuck Green Day, they're sellouts." It's 2008, it's been a really long time. But at the time it was '95, and everyone was so angry, saying, "Oh my god punk rock is becoming mainstream what are we going to do?" Yeah, well, shit happens and we needed to learn who was fake and who was not.

And that's what inspired me to write: writing about punk, interviewing bands. Then I started writing about my own experiences, after reading more personal zines, and books too. Dorothy Allison I loved, JD Salinger, Cometbus, *Doris*, *Absolutely Zippo*, *Emergency Zine*. It's funny because I was never into comics, but since I liked drawing I was always like, "I might as well illustrate my stories." And that's still what I'm doing now, writing and then drawing based on the writing. I usually write first and then draw.

Margaret: *I'm trying to explore what it means to be both an anarchist and fiction writer...*

Cristy: I guess when I was 17 or 18 and I started doing Food Not Bombs and working with the Coalition of Immokalee Workers in south Florida. I was working with a lot of the migrant farm workers who are way underpaid. I was becoming an activist outside of my brain, outside of creating art. And by being more involved in the world, I started thinking about my identity: who fucked me over, why am I the way I am, why were Green Day the only people who understood me when I was 14? They were writing these songs questioning religion, sexuality.

And having radical beliefs is really what made me want to create anything at all. I can't just write about bands for the rest of my life. So when I was older and started getting involved in movements that weren't necessarily just art and music, started seeing other people doing things, I decided I wanted to do those things too. And I wanted to write about it. Experience it and then write about it. A lot of my zines were just me documenting protests, Food Not Bombs, my community. I'd write about how you can exist as a queer person in an anarchist community that is mostly straight, or as a person of color in an anarchist community that is mostly white. Challenging all of those ideas, that's really what got me writing a lot. Those were the last issues of my zine.

And then that just kind of snowballed into writing what I'm writing about now. *Bad Habits* is about existing in the world as young and messed up and confused, post-activist I guess. It's about leaving your community because you feel crazy and depressed and suicidal and you start doing a bunch of drugs. How do you rebuild yourself? How can you be that really radical, awesome, strong person that you were before you fell apart? And what made you fall apart? Was it the community you were in? Was it abuse? So what I'm writing now is about human experiences, like love, about rebuilding your body after abuse. Of course there's the constant questioning of why do we live in this society that makes it so fucking hard to call out someone who's been violent in a sexual relationship? Why do we live in a society where it is so hard to be bipolar and be seen as normal? I still want to write about society and how it hurts us, but I'm not really writing about protests anymore. I mean, I may, who knows, but this is about *Bad Habits*, my most recent piece of work.

Margaret: *In* Bad Habits, *you dealt with sexuality in a very mature way, talking about how it can be both positive and negative. I feel like that balance isn't present in most writing about sex, particularly fictional and particularly illustrated. Actually, it was kind of embarrassing reading the book in a public setting...*

Cristy: I know! When I first got it and I was like, "Oh I wanna look through it every day," cause it's my baby, you know? And I was riding the bus and I was like, "Oh that's a blowjob, I gotta cover that part, oh there's boobs there..." But yeah, how can you live in the world and be a sexual person, although that is such a stigmatized thing, especially as a woman? How can you use sex to heal from fucked up sex?

Margaret: *One of the things that you're known for is illustrating body types outside our culture's standard of beauty, and I was wondering how conscious that decision was?*

Cristy: It's funny, because my entire life I've just been drawing my friends or people who want to be drawn, or people who I think are awesome. My reality isn't all these "flawless" people. There are a lot of awesome women illustrators, and men too, who are putting really intense ideas out there, yet all the people they're drawing have perfect boobs, are really small and Barbie looking. That's fine too, I've drawn thin people with perfect boobs before, but it's not really the focus, the focus is just people in general. Who's to say what kind of boobs are perfect? It's just annoying. There are a lot of illustrators who they themselves are really awesome radical people with really awesome ideas but they're still submitting to this standard of beauty in art, like in the Renaissance, but it's not the Renaissance anymore.

Anything could be beautiful if it's drawn... I love old things, old cities. Looking at something and observing it and seeing what you love about it and then implementing that into a piece of art it can glorify anything. Anything can be glorified through art, which I always felt is what made art a powerful tool. Showing bodies that are considered imperfect, transforming what would be imperfect into a beautiful image. Also, it helps to be attracted to things that are conventionally imperfect.

Margaret: *I think that ties into what you write about. I think that a lot of radical people will glorify their subjects, but you write about real people...*

Cristy: With issues.

Margaret: *Yeah.*

Cristy: *Bad Habits* is very autobiographical. It's fictionalized, but a lot of the things that I write about are things that I've experienced, that I've felt, that would be considered bad choices. But humans make bad choices. There was this review of the book that I read from a very liberal webpage. It was very, "This is just glorifying young people who are messed up. It's another woman whining about her irresponsibilities." Instead of realizing it was about a woman discussing abusive relationships, it was like, "God, get over your ex-boyfriend." It was very unfair and fucked up, but that's the way society thinks. Nobody wants to hear things that they see in themselves. I like to write about things the way that they are. Being in love with someone who is kinda an asshole. Everyone has been in love with someone who is kind of an asshole. And for the rest of your life you're going to be like, "Well that was my first love." I still fall in love with assholes all the time.

Anything could be beautiful if it's drawn. Looking at something and observing it and seeing what you love about it and then implementing that into a piece of art it can glorify anything.

I guess my goal would be to just show, to humanize the fact that we're all kind of messed up and that we're all going to make mistakes. We should persecute each other when we don't own up to our mistakes. But if we *do* own up to our mistakes, we should talk about it and grow.

Margaret: *The format of the story itself is non-traditional, especially with the way you intersperse illustration. It definitely seems like a novel born of the per-zine [personal zine] tradition. Was writing the book unconventionally a conscious choice?*

Cristy: I never went to school for writing. I mean, I read books. I love Tom Robbins, but I knew I wasn't going to rewrite *Still Life With Woodpecker*. But I spent most of my life writing short stories that were written in a very grammatically incorrect way. A lot of my influences were songwriters. I grew up listening to Green Day and Crimpshrine, and just being like, "Oh my god, these are the best lyrics I'm going to write a story that sounds just like these lyrics." I use a lot of fragments, a lot of paragraphs that are just one sentence fragment and then a new paragraph. Just expressing what I need to say in the way that I'm thinking it. And the book went through so much editing. I didn't know how to use semi-colons, I used the word frivolous like a million times on one page...

> I didn't want to do a comic. I'd like to, but I don't like drawing people having dialogue. I just want to draw people ripping out their insides and people having sex... I don't want to draw people talking or walking.

Margaret: *Frivolously?*

Cristy: Yeah. I used it frivolously. It was awesome to work with a publisher who edits. It went through five rounds of editing. But it was good. Now the book is in chronological order, but when I first handed it into them, they asked me, "Why are you talking about being a 15 year-old here and then being a 20-year old before?" It was written like, "Short story, short story, short story," and then I got help putting it all together. The writing didn't change at all really; it was mostly structural changes. I was called out on sentences that made absolutely no sense, and I got rid of a lot of those. *Bad Habits* was the first book that went through that process.

Indestructible, which I put out before—which is about growing up in Miami as a teenager—was edited for misspelled words and sentences that *really* didn't make sense. But I read it now and I'm just like, "I don't know what the fuck I'm talking about here." I don't want to change that book or anything, I like that it's a little imperfect. But that one feels more like a zine. It's a bunch of consistent short stories that all have something to do with each other, and are chronologically placed, but they don't read as a narrative.

This is the first book that I've written where things pop up in the end that were brought up in the beginning. It's still not traditionally presented. I didn't want to do a comic. I'd like to, but I don't like drawing people having dialogue. I just want to draw people ripping out their insides and people having sex... I don't want to draw people talking or walking. But I will, I need to develop my skills. I want to do a full graphic novel someday. But for now, I was really inspired by *Cruddy*, by Lindy Berry, and *Blood & Guts in High School* by Kathy Acker.

Margaret: *So do you think that there's something positive to be said about having this other group of people going through your work before they publish it?*

Cristy: Yeah, because the people who were editing, they know where I'm coming from. They've read all the same zines I've read. One of the editors was my age. It's just that he went to school for writing. Both of the editors, they've been doing what they're doing for so long, but they work for this indie press that's really into putting out work that other people don't want to put out. A lot of other publishers that we sent the book to, the editors were into it, the young editors, but the bosses were like, "This is too edgy, we don't want to put it out, no one will buy it." But the people at Soft Skull are down. And they always ask for my approval before they make changes. It was a really positive experience because it was all constructive criticism, and no one was like, "This part of the book isn't important," or "Why do you have to say this?" It was a good editing process.

Margaret: *Do you feel like something can be accomplished, as a writer, not just from a purely literary standpoint, but in terms of things like effecting social change?*

Cristy: I'm at a point where I'm not as involved in as many local groups and organizations as I used to be. I want to, and my brain is getting a little more functional again, but for the past 3 years I've just been writing and drawing. I still get the same response to my work that's like, "This piece of writing helped me deal with my assault, helped me deal with coming out to my family." And that's why I'm doing what I'm doing. If nobody saw the political context or the message behind my stories, I'd probably just get bored. You don't just want to be an entertainer the rest of your life. I'm really grateful that people identify with it.

I like to write about things the way that they are. Being in love with someone who is kinda an asshole. Everyone has been in love with someone who is kind of an asshole. I still fall in love with assholes all the time.

But I don't really like to write about my situation as though I'm perfect at dealing with it. Obviously, if you read *Bad Habits*, you'll learn that I'm not really skilled at dealing with a lot things, especially getting broken up with. I want to write about things we all persecute ourselves for doing, but I want to write about them and let people know they don't need to persecute themselves. Ⓐ

"An awful lot of words have been written. I don't think we need any more words to know that we need to stop this nightmare around us."

—Octavio Buenaventura

OCTAVIO BUENAVENTURA

Now here is an author shrouded from public view. Originally published by The International Anarchist Conspiracy, Octavio Buenaventura is the author of the genuinely amazing occult novella Ever & Anon. *The International Anarchist Conspiracy is itself a pseudo-fictional entity, a propaganda arm that publishes communiqués and theory that are a sort of magical realism superimposed onto reality. No one can tell if they're joking.*

I let some travelers from Washington know that I was looking for Octavio. "Never heard of him," they told me, "but we'll ask around." Some weeks later, an email. Not from Octavio, but from the Ministry of Secrets of the International Anarchist Conspiracy. As requested, I forwarded questions along.

He told me about the power of myth and fiction, about better uses for words than books.

Margaret: *I'll start with a nice, broad question. Why do you write fiction?*

Octavio: I will answer all of these questions badly.

I write fiction because I have nothing to do with my spare time. When I fall into the repetitiveness of my supposedly radical lifestyle, spinning fantasies is the only way I can feel content with a life spent largely in stasis. I value my fantasies, but they serve largely as a complex rationalization of my inability to act. They are strange side-effects of my impatience for a world in which our collective fantasies are our own lives. A world that words cannot create but merely represent.

Fiction is everywhere. The most powerful creators of fiction are the governments and corporations of the world. Their fictions are meant to enslave massive amounts of people, binding them to a product, a ministry, a people, a symbol, a country. These fictions flow through our minds constantly. The fact that we are numb to these saturation techniques is proof of this. We are all familiar with the slow, consistent narratives that are spun through advertising and propaganda.

But what awful fictions they are. They are revolting. They make your mind sick. You begin to emulate zombies when you emulate their stories, when you believe in their myths, when you swim within their narrative of chains. They make people obese and turn them into cybernetic killers. They strip away people's souls and turn them into puppets of ecstatic marketers and grinning counter-intelligence operatives. These fictions are powerful in their scope, not in their effect.

The fictions of those who have escaped their narrative are far more resilient and alive. I will not list which fictions these are. If you are reading this obscure book, there are fictions which have stayed with you forever, fictions that keep you connected to a time or a place or people. The fiction created together by a community of free people is a fiction that is not susceptible to fire.

In my impatience and inability to act, I choose to write my own fictions and give them to people.

Margaret: *So, part of what you're saying, perhaps, is that we can tell other stories, other fictions and myths, to counter the ones that mainstream culture insists upon?*

Octavio: Yes, we can. But they will still only be our stories. If they are understood as such (stories, fiction, fantasies), they can do no damage. I think a story which becomes a law is a nightmare, a deranged fantasy. These nightmares, like the one we are currently living in, become genocidal and start to metastasize. These nightmares cannot tolerate the existence of other stories.

And so the creation of stories is absolutely essential to resisting the nightmarish monoculture. Without them, we slip back into their celluloid dreamland. Sometimes, when we try to think of new stories, we have nothing to draw upon aside from what we have learned from decades of their media saturation. I value my fantasies, but they serve largely as a complex rationalization of my inability to act. Their books, their movies, their news, their images, their lies. Sometimes, we weave the nightmare without realizing it. It is all we have known. Escape is difficult.

A total escape leads to a destruction of all representation. This is something people cannot imagine. How does one abandon all they have learned? That is the question. We merry artists are stuck in this wasteland. This desolate expanse of wreckage and repetition. These are questions we all have to answer.

Some idiots have made their art subservient to the Party. Others have made their art subservient to the coin. If we make our art subservient to no one, who does it serve? Why are we not writing books that must be burnt by those in power? Why are fascists not attacking our galleries? When will we begin to use our gifts to fight? [Antonin] Artaud called it all pig shit. It is all pig shit unless it is not all pig shit. And it all seems like pig shit right now.

Our era is the era of juxtaposition. We can see a picture of a charred baby in Gaza while at the same time listen to a beautiful song our friend made. All atrocity, all genocide, all horror is given the same level of importance as a painting or a blog. All are seen as one giant, golden, glowing ball of pig shit. Everyone puts headphones in their ears and stretches their canvases and knows that burning white death is falling onto schools while they go to the bar or watch a movie. The horror is known and it is accepted because at least, at least, at least there is beauty, beauty, beauty.

Margaret: *What do you think that radical fiction writers, yourself and others, can do? How can we be useful? Do we need to be useful through our fiction, or are the ideas divorced from one another?*

Octavio: I would like to think that we can be useful. Perhaps we can be of some use right now. I pretend that my words can be of some use. I know that I have been deeply affected by other people's art and writing.

At this point in time, however, a lot of words have been written. There are an awful lot of them. I don't think we need any more words to know that we need to stop this nightmare around us. Words seem to only push our actions off into the future. But in the darkness they are very nice to have. Our words are burning veins of memory stretching away in every direction, carrying with them lessons from other times and places and people. These words can only keep us content for so long,

Sometimes, when we try to think of new stories, we have nothing to draw upon aside from what we have learned from decades of their media saturation. Their books, their movies, their news, their images, their lies. Sometimes, we weave the nightmare without realizing it. It is all we have known.

though, before becoming a fetish. This culture creates fetishes out of everything.

One way for artists to be useful is to throw themselves through plate glass windows and write *fuck you* on the sides of buildings. Paint your misery on peoples' white picket fences and write pornography inside Christmas cards. Take none of your creations seriously. Because they are not serious things, they are toilet paper and fire starter and garbage. So stuff that garbage into a cop's mouth or into the machine's databases. Refuse to speak their language. Learn to see without seeing.

Margaret: *One thing that I've found to be curious, for myself, is to be a creator of cultural artifacts, when at the same time I'm very influenced by immediatist, anti-art critiques. I like this idea of saying, "We make these things, and perhaps they're important, but you know what? What if they're not?"*

Octavio: If one person I love likes what create I am happy. My creations are important to me. If others find them important, I care very little.

These things we make have real importance within small circles. Outside of that circle, they get picked up and tossed around by the ebbs and flows of the ruler's broken machine, thus losing all of their power and becoming empty shells.

A dying child in Gaza has no care for my creations, nor should she.

Margaret: *Your novella,* Ever & Anon, *takes place in a post-revolutionary society. But unlike perhaps any other post-revolutionary fiction I've read, it isn't about the revolution or the post-revolutionary society, as much as it is about the characters, philosophy, and magic. I appreciated that. It felt honestly like fiction, and not propaganda...*

Octavio: Firstly, I would like to clarify that, from what I understand, the International Anarchist Conspiracy is attempting to mirror the structures of power it wishes to destroy. They are also making fools of themselves. In my opinion, this de-legitimizes anyone else who attempts to act in a similar manner. Because anyone else doing the same thing would look like either another fool or a fascist.

The IAC insisted on placing their logo on the back of my novella. I cared little and said, "Okay," knowing that what they were calling propaganda was not propaganda. I am relieved that you found fiction within its covers.

Ever & Anon was meant to be a portrait of a problem I have imagined. What will happen to the "unique ones," the fire bringers, the "black brothers," and the wild at heart in a post-revolutionary situation? Where do they go? These people I am describing are people who make waves and cause trouble, people who cannot help their destructive impulses and will dive straight into the sun. The entire novella was meant to shed light on this little conundrum.

The plot is simple. Three artists live in two houses in the snowy mountains above a town in a post-revolutionary setting. The artists are supported by the town below and regularly exchange their art for food and luxuries. One day, one of the characters finds that her painting has manifested itself in front of her eyes, without her will behind it. She does not know why five marbles have suddenly appeared in her wall and can find no explanation. This causes her to begin to question everything about art, reality, and reason. In the process, much chaos is wrought on the two houses in the mountains.

I should also add that the book started off as a short story with no direction, originally meant to be a present to a loved one, which it still is.

In the process of describing the journey of the three artists, I inadvertently began writing about the entire development of Western culture and how it influenced them. This led back to the myths and gods of Greece and Babylon. The largest fictions, the myths and the gods, do not die quickly. The entire novella describes the process of these fictions being understood for what they are: _____ [Octavio left these blanks intentionally in his letters to me]. The characters plunge into the abyss and find themselves surrounded by fire when they emerge from it. All myths burn at the end of *Ever & Anon*. Their power returns to it source:_____. The fictions all grow small again.

Here is a partial list of the myths and gods and fictions that burn at the end of the book: rationality, reason, domestication, slavery, Man, Woman, the Mono, the One, the future, representation, and fascism. Power does not burn. Power is only a word expressing one thing: magic. Another word for magic is:_____. Magic without the One, or God, is the magic of the future described in *Ever & Anon*. Magic without a center, a magic with practices and rituals that change each day. Magic no book can contain, no matter how red and white and black it pages might be. Each of the three characters attempt to channel their gifts into fixed forms and find those forms incapable of holding _____. Their efforts to do so drive them mad.

The post-revolutionary setting was necessary, because this sort of implosion which the protagonists feel can only occur when the entire system has crashed and the fictions of the twisted masters no longer influence anyone. My concern was not the details of the future society but the problem I have described above. A poet should not attempt to meddle in affairs of which they are ignorant.

Margaret: *In your piece and in the non-fiction that your publishers put out, myth and magic are heavily interlaced into anarchist struggle. What can you tell me about that? How do they relate?*

Octavio: That's an interesting question. I'll talk about the International Anarchist Conspiracy first.

They seem to be interested in writing children's stories. Or at least that's what I think. They use the word "magic" to describe things which are mostly physical and visibly direct in nature. Once they called it physically altering one's surrounding. I call that acting, they call it magic. As far as some people are concerned, it's a complete joke. However, I am under the suspicion that something is being withheld from view by the Ministry. They are not telling the full truth. But they are also not lying about the correlations they are drawing between certain things. I don't know the cipher. Maybe there isn't one, but I think they are trying to render all methods of fixed, thought-organization systems obsolete. For all of their secrecy, they seem to really hate it.

Anarchism and magic forged a connection long before the International Anarchist Conspiracy sensationalized that connection and before there was a Hakim Bey or a Starhawk. A friend once said that perhaps it was because of the letter A. I believe anarchism, which does not seek to have any form of hierarchy, goes against the beliefs of many people interested in magic. Many people interested in magic do not wish to live in a world without the amplifiers of civilization. Some of them are currently filling this civilization's many leadership roles. There are many contradictions with anarchism and magic as it has been known.

The two belief systems, however, annihilate one another in a grand synthesis, the results of which can already be seen if one knows what to look for. Anarchism-the-mother and Magic-the-father create the future. Magic frees the mind from slavery and anarchism frees the body from slavery. Some people call magic the reconciling of opposites. Anarchism is the same thing. It is bringing those who once preyed on each other together for the purpose of living in balance.

Some magicians are not interested in balance, however. These perverted, power-addicted magicians have created their own destruction through their sickening practices. Whether they are aware of this or not is irrelevant. A world without their concentration camps and mushroom clouds is approaching. It has been approaching since Emma Goldman read Nietzsche, since the tribes of Germania fought the Romans, since Greece began to burn with rage.

On a side note, the new sell-all phrase for Macy's is: "The magic of Macy's."

Nestor Mahkno was more powerful than any fat Magus in England. Emma Goldman had more fire in her body than all of the Queens of England put together. They received their power from the places they fought for and the people they loved. Queen Elizabeth was an intoxicated faerie turning everything beautiful and free into gold for her rings. There were free women in the Ukraine who could turn Elizabeth inside out, women who will never be written about or remembered. Anarchists are practitioners with no knowledge of any existing craft. Anarchists invent their own practice, their own craft. And they are all the better for it. Ⓐ

"I was attracted to Fantasy originally because it wasn't a defined genre. Like rock and roll, you could make something of your own out of it. If I was a young writer today, I'd have absolutely nothing to do with it."

—Michael Moorcock

MICHAEL MOORCOCK

I feel like it's safe to say that Michael Moorcock has written more books than the rest of the authors I interviewed for this project combined. An exact number is actually hard to come by, but I counted 108 novels, novellas, and graphic novels on one bibliography. And more than a few of these books explore explicitly anarchist themes. I'd read some of his sword and sorcery novels before, but I picked up the Nomad In The Time Streams *series a few years back and read a parable about black power and a story about Makhno and Stalin fighting side-by-side (and of course, against one another). Airships and anarchists; you really can't go wrong. Moorcock has been hugely influential on modern society, albeit most of that has been secondhand. My personal favorite revelation is that he created the chaos symbol that so many of my friends have tattooed.*

I'd spoken to Michael briefly a few years back for the first issue of SteamPunk Magazine, *and it was a pleasure to get to pick his brain again, this time about his anarchism, about what he's accomplished, and how angry he is with the people who have watered-down his ideas.*

Margaret: *You once described Nestor Makhno as "a martyr to a cause that can never be lost but which the world may never properly understand." Referring, of course, to anarchism... you've stated yourself at various points in your life as an anarchist, and I was wondering if you could tell us about what that means to you?*

Michael: I'm an anarchist and a pragmatist. My moral/philosophical position is that of an anarchist. This makes it very easy for me to make a decision from what you might call a Kropotkinist point of view. There's been so little good experience of anarchists running big cities that I'd love to see the experiment-made. So far anarchism has only apparently worked well in rural environments.

This was certainly true of Makhno. I like him because he stuck, as far as we can tell, rigorously to his anarchist principles.

Margaret: *What I've set out to explore with this project is what it means to be both an anarchist and a fiction writer. How do you think the two relate, at least in your life?*

Michael: My books frequently deal with aristocratic heroes, gods and so forth. All of them end on a note which often states quite baldly that one should serve neither gods nor masters but become one's own master. This is a constant theme throughout all my fiction. Philosophically I, together with my protagonists (where I identify with them) seek to find a balance between Law and Chaos. Frequently my characters achieve that balance by refusing to serve anything but their own consciences. The books, of course, are written on many levels and I'm talking mostly about what you might call my romances or "entertainments"—popular fiction addressing, I hope, intelligent people who have reasonably open minds. I find such readers are well represented on my website. Several are committed anarchists.

The whole point of my fiction is to allow readers to decide for themselves their own moral attitudes. My stories refuse to "guide" the reader in any direction. I try to set out the material and let them decide what they think.

Margaret: *And how did you get into anarchism personally?*

Michael: Being around anarchists. Listening to old guys at the Malatesta Club talking about the Spanish Civil War. Reading. I've been attracted to anarchist ideas since I was 17. But it took me a while to become a sophisticated political thinker, thanks mostly to reading Kropotkin.

Margaret: You've been known to incorporate historical anarchists into your novels, particularly Nestor Makhno. Aside from making your novels that much more engaging to those of us familiar with him, what purposes led you to this?

Michael: I like to introduce as many readers as possible to my heroes. Many readers have written to me and told me they had never heard of Makhno, Bakunin, Kropotkin, and the rest and I've been able to point them to, say, [George] Woodcock's *Anarchism* [an introduction to anarchist history].

Margaret: I'm excited to include you in this project, by the way. One of the first things I did when I started this project was to re-read "Starship Stormtroopers," [Michael Moorcock's 1978 essay about political science fiction in general and Robert Heinlein in specific] which I feel like was one of the first things to draw the connections between anti-authoritarianism and science fiction. How do you think things have changed since you wrote that?

Michael: Heinlein, like a lot of Americans, was a right libertarian. I have something in common with right libertarians but of course I have much more in common with left libertarians!

I believe that many of these libertarians are essentially authoritarians, though I respect those who see the Constitution as the law to live by. This, of course, allows them to carry massive firepower. My argument against this is that if you don't own a nuke, you don't have equal firepower with a potentially repressive government. I like the ending of Alfred Bester's (libertarian) *Tiger, Tiger!* or *The Stars My Destination* [the book was published under both names at various points], in which the power to destroy the universe is put into the hands of every individual. A great ideal but, of course, it doesn't allow for the suicidal psychopath who'd quite happily destroy himself and everyone else. I'm not sure I like the thought of that psychopath being able to destroy the world, but I like the underlying moral idea of everyone being responsible for the existence of the world. I don't think we had thought about suicide bombers of a religious persuasion when I wrote that piece!

Margaret: *What do you think you have accomplished, or could hope to accomplish, in the social or political sphere, with your fiction, or as a fiction writer?*

Michael: I've introduced a lot of readers to anarchism and I've helped, according to their letters, a lot more think for themselves. The whole point of my fiction is to allow readers to decide for themselves their own moral attitudes. The Jerry Cornelius stories, for instance, are pure anarchism in their refusal to "guide" the reader in any direction. I try to set out the material and let them decide what they think. I think I've encouraged readers to do that and several writers have been influenced by me to try the same sort of techniques.

Margaret: *I am fascinated by the influence you've had on our culture. For example, a lot of your concepts, from the Law vs. Chaos dichotomy to potions of speed, were adopted into the very beginning of Dungeons & Dragons, which in turn has influenced an ever-growing number of fantasy games. Of course, sometimes it seems that people just emulate the surface of things and miss a lot of the underlying philosophy. How do you feel about that?*

Michael: I'm disappointed when people pick up on the ideas superficially. My theory of the multiverse, where I coined the term (unconscious of William James coining it to explain multiple ways of thinking/being) wasn't just a handy way for explaining why Superman stories were contradictory. The book—my first SF book—described a complex idea which, I'm glad to say, has been taken up by theoretical physicists rather more profoundly than by most comics and other popular fiction/drama. I'm irritated when people use my images/ideas/characters to plunge the genre straight back into all the crap I was trying to confront. My books are fundamentally about fantasy and how it's used, what it does. The underlying message is always—confront reality. If these tools (the ones I've created or adapted) are useful to you in order to do that, so much the better. However, when people build on my ideas or are inspired by them to do their own original work, I celebrate. Alan Moore, for instance, gives me credit but is himself an enormously influential and original writer. That makes me proud and makes me want to publicize such work whenever I come across it, just as I like it when people make use of Jerry Cornelius [Moorock's repeating character] to tell their own stories, make their own points. People who realize, as M. John Harrison pointed out, that Jerry is as much a technique as he is a character.

I'm not for censorship but I am for strategies which marginalise stuff that works to objectify women and suggests women enjoy being beaten.

What also depresses me, incidentally, is when books like *Mother London* or the Pyat books are perceived as fantasy. They are not. I don't see the Cornelius books in that way, either. They were not originally seen like this by critics or the public. I want people to understand that these books are confrontational, about reality. They're not escapist fantasy. I get particularly pissed off by people describing the Pyat books as "alternate realities." They are about real events, real people, real issues, about this world and our responsibility for it. That the narrator fantasies about his lack of responsibility is one of the issues. Similarly, I have written sophisticated narratives, like the Blood trilogy, which describe the philosophical (if you like) structure of what I call Law and Chaos.

I'm frankly contemptuous of people who trivialize my ideas when they rip them off.

Margaret: *One of the things that I've observed among a lot of anarchist writers (and other interesting writers too, of course) is the idea of the anti-hero, something which really turns most genre fiction on its head. I like how, as you mentioned, this leaves the reader without an external moral compass. Care to elaborate?*

Michael: I'm concerned with helping, I hope, the reader determine their own moral compass.

The anti-hero is traditionally one who stands against all received morality, all received opinion. He confronts society and refuses its unexamined assumptions. This is why I find myself at odds with certain middle-class writers, no matter how good. Like, for instance the late John Updike. I remember him writing a phrase that went, "You know how girls smell in autumn..." Assuming that everyone shares certain perceptions. Well, I don't bloody know how girls smell in autumn and I don't know what it's like to grow up in a conventional middle-class environment like Iain McEwan or even Martin Amis. I have almost nothing in common with those people. I have more in common with the writers Iain Sinclair also celebrates, like Jack Trevor Story or Gerald Kersh, who are "forgotten" by the literary world—marginalized at least—precisely because they don't know how girls smell in autumn, either.

Margaret: *You've written a fair amount of criticism of the fantasy genre, and never shied away from understanding the way an author's politics influence their fiction. Have you noticed any current trends, politically or philosophically speaking, in the genre?*

Michael: I read almost no fantasy, especially generic fantasy, so I can't really comment. Generic fiction almost by definition reflects—whatever it is—social fiction, historical fiction, thrillers, whatever—social norms and conventional ideas. Most fantasy and SF is vaguely liberal, some of it is disturbingly right wing, written by people who like the idea of slicing other people's heads off and so on. I was attracted to it originally because it wasn't a defined genre, there was very little of it and, like rock and roll, you could make something of your own out of it. If I was a young writer today, I'd have absolutely nothing to do with it. Of course there are going to be some good writers who put their own stamp on things or write essentially outside genre (Jonathan Carroll, Jeff Ford, Mike Harrison, Jeff Vander-Meer spring to mind) and some of these have what I'd call an anarchist sensibility—Harrison in particular. I like how Ballard has carved himself an original, bloody-minded, socially critical form out of what was originally just outstandingly good generic SF. And Burroughs, of course, remains a great inspiration.

Margaret: *And a final question: I've heard that you worked to get John Norman's women-as-slaves Gor series kept out of the young-adult section of bookstores?*

Michael: I suggested that Smith's [a London newstand chain] put them on the top shelves along with the other stuff they thought should go up there. I'm not for censorship but I am for strategies which marginalize stuff that works to objectify women and suggests women enjoy being beaten. Ⓐ

"The ideal artist is somebody who deals with day-to-day events. They're going to have a lot more genuine and interesting things to say when they're immersed in the world instead of cutting themselves off from it."

—Carissa van den Berk Clark

CARISSA VAN DEN BERK CLARK

Carissa van den Berk Clark's book Yours For The Revolution *was probably the first DIY-published novel I saw in an infoshop when I got into politics. It wasn't until years later that I discovered its sequel,* May it Come Quickly Like a Shaft Sundering in the Dark.

I tracked her down for this project and it turns out she, by joy and by occupation, is an anarchist social worker. We spoke about how best to write earnestly, about the role of the artist and the anarchist in the greater social struggle, and about riotgrrl.

Margaret: *So you've published two novels,* Yours for the Revolution, *and its sequel* May it Come Quickly Like a Shaft Sundering in the Dark. *Both deal rather explicitly with squatters and freight trains and punks and gender politics and all of that. Although the setting is clearly fictional, it seems pretty clear that you are or were immersed in that counterculture...*

Carissa: I've been a part of movements for change, whether to resist war, stop racism, redistribute wealth and power, since I was 15 and I don't see myself changing. I honestly hope I never do. I think this is important, for a number of reasons. One of the most important is that my fiction has anarchist values, which for me include social and economic equality. The other is that I think one should write what one knows, otherwise she or he has to rely on stereotypes. There's something very uncomfortable about writing in stereotypes and it's always felt ethically uncomfortable to me. This ethical dilemma has a strong influence on my writing and on the way I live my life.

Margaret: *I've read a fair amount of fiction about travel culture and/or anarchism and/or rebellion that is really clearly written by an outsider. And usually it ends up offending or annoying me, actually.*

Carissa: Right, it either offends you or it's just somehow not a very interesting story. It's very surface-y. There is a difference between a literary piece that really moves you and changes the way you think and a story that merely distracts you from day-to-day life.

Margaret: *A lot of those stories, the ones written by outsiders, just present us as stereotypes.*

Carissa: And they don't get into the personal relationships that exist, because unless you're in the middle of it, you don't really see people as people. You create these images of what you think they are... it's just one-dimensional.

Margaret: *So it seems like one of the reasons that we should be writing fiction is because people are going to mythologize us, since we live differently, so maybe it makes sense that we are the ones to present that.*

Carissa: I wasn't particularly worried about people mythologizing anarchists. I honestly never thought about it. I really just wanted to show that we have the potential to be like the Haymarket anarchists and all the massive political coalitions that came about alongside of them and that, if we do, we can get hurt. The book tries to show how governments actually hamper democracy rather than promote it. Anarchists today unfortunately isolate themselves pretty badly and they weren't portrayed that way in the novel.

Margaret: *For a long time, we anarchists have been talking about how, politically, we shouldn't be isolating ourselves. But it's interesting to me because, as a writer, it's very important to understand how so many different people work. The same skill applies to both actions.*

Carissa: Exactly, and I have seen how important it is for us anarchists to work more intimately with our communities. When I was writing *Yours for the Revolution* and its sequel, I was much more involved in political protests and organizing demonstrations, and much of that work was done exclusively with other anarchist and activist types. When I started writing my third book, *Who's Esperenza?*, a bunch of us in St. Louis had gotten together and started a non-profit and basically used that non-profit to do a community land trust and bought a building and used it as a community space.

Two things were interesting about this. One, the non-profit organized using an anarchist model, which is kinda a new thing... no one was organizing non-profits on anarchist models, but why couldn't you? You can organize it however you want to, since it's not like you're doing it to make money. And then the second thing is because there were actually a couple of us anarchist social workers around, we came up with the radical social worker anarchist model. We focused on saying, "Look, this isn't just going to be a community of anarchists. We need to have people on the board who live in this neighborhood, we need to knock on all the doors and ask what people would like to see here." And that's precisely what happened.

An afterschool youth program was the result. And it was great because the way you get the community involved is by interacting with their children. When the kids were there, their parents showed up. And suddenly there were these amazing bridges being built between anarchist kids who usually only hung out around each other and these community groups that were suddenly becoming educated about different ways of resisting, of different organizing models. It was great to see that, and that's something that I see as becoming more and more important in terms of where the anarchist movement should go. We have more leverage than we think, in our small numbers, in the urban cities where we usually live. A lot of times we could do a lot more.

Margaret: *So you published your two books through a record label...*

Carissa: Through Bloodlink. Actually, I published one through Bloodlink. When I wrote *Yours for the Revolution*, and actually the other one was done at that time too, I didn't really want to spend much time shopping it around; I felt that it was kinda necessary that it come out right away, because it fit the politics of the time. When it was put out it was basically right after 9-11. If I'd had to shop it around for a year or two, the issues would still be relevant, but they'd kind of already be done.

We decided to cut the whole story into two books because of the cost. We could sell it for much cheaper, and it would give me more time to edit through the second part. It was nice also because the second part came out right after the Iraq war started. It worked really well as a sequel, and I got to change things along with current events. Since printing each one was cheaper, I could sell them for $5, which was something I'd wanted to do so that anyone could get it. Books are so expensive, and it winds up that people read less because it just costs so much more to get a book then get a movie. I also wanted the writing to carry the reader through the story almost like they were watching a movie. I wanted a book that people would stay up all night reading because they just couldn't sleep, wondering what would happen next.

The book that I'm in the process of writing, that I'm taking my time with, it's basically a take-off of Ayn Rand's novels, but it will teach the opposite story. It's based on *Atlas Shrugged*, about railroads, and it's basically about a bunch of anarchists and workers taking over a railroad line. It focuses on community vs. individual, just as her books did, but it does it from an anarchist perspective.

Margaret: *I watched a documentary about Ayn Rand recently, and I remember thinking that about a quarter of what she says made so much sense, and then she undermined it with all of this...*

Carissa: She's a social Darwinist and a narcissist. The Bush Administration and many of these Chicago school economists who left us in the mess we're in, loved her. Rand's theories were also very appealing to libertarians. She advocated the individual over society which is essentially an American ideal, which has been very harmful to Americans through corporate greed, family dysfunction, heightened crime, and decreased neighborhood cohesion.

Ayn Rand is confusing, just as the idea of libertarianism is confusing. As Americans, it is hard to imagine anything involving individualism can be negative. What they don't realize is that in the US, many of our problems, like our non-existent social safety net, lack of unions, non-existent left, AIG bonuses, are in a large part due to our overemphasis of the individual at the expense of the community.

Margaret: *You often mix fiction and non-fiction together. What draws you to that? It seems like a lot of the anarchist writers*

I've spoken to do this. A lot of people fictionalize real things, or present real things as fiction.

Carissa: When I was 17 and writing zines, I was very influenced by Henry Miller's style of writing. The way that Miller detailed human emotion and struggle and made them into an art form was inspiring to me. This style of writing essentially requires mixing non-fiction with fiction because you have to actually experience the emotion in order to trigger it in others.

Miller wrote a book about writing where he described his writing process: when he was writing, he would focus on specific times in his life or people he loved or towns he lived in that really emotionally resonated. He would try to write about them with as much detail and emotion as possible. He found that when he did that, he was able to find his true voice. I essentially do the same thing. I start with my own tragedies, heartbreaks, love stories, friendships, and then add fictional layers on top.

> When people are treated badly for a certain amount of time, and they have to hold it in? It accumulates, and it isn't pretty afterwards. You just have to deal with that.

Margaret: *Maybe this gets at one advantage that anarchists might have as fiction writers. A lot of youth anarchist culture is very travel-oriented, and it's about encountering new things and exploring new ideas. At its best, of course.*

Carissa: We're coming from the vantage point of being at a low social-economic level but are often very highly educated (by either formal or informal education). We also actively advocate for human equality and try to fight oppression wherever we go. We thus have a specific standpoint that we come from, and it's a very interesting, valuable standpoint.

Margaret: *You used to run a zine for a long time,* Screams From the Inside. *What kind of differences did you find between writing a zine versus writing a book?*

Carissa: The zine started as punk music focused (band interviews, reviews), then became political and social commentary then became a grouping of short stories. I enjoyed writing short stories but kept thinking, I wonder if I could write a book? I wondered, "Am I smart enough to do this?" Well, who knows if I'll ever be smart enough, but I pulled it off anyway. While it's gotten a lot of criticism, and the first one has so many editing problems, its publication made me realize that many of life hurdles are not such a big deal if you just work on them slowly, day by day. Before you know it, you have an entire book written.

Margaret: *Do you think there's any hope for impacting the world through fiction?*

Carissa: I think it's the same kind of hope that there is for any kind of art. But you need a combination of a lot of things. Fiction isn't just gonna change everything. What I like about fiction is that you can create a story that people can emotionally resonate with, that they can relate to. It's different than other kinds of art forms. To me, it seemed like a very good way of explaining a point of view or a way of looking at the world. The messages I've tried to communicate have been: one, we're all in this together; two, that governments, especially large governments, basically exist to protect the rich and powerful; three, we are the only ones who are able to change the conditions that oppress us; and four, that we are able to create our own types of societal structures.

I wanted the books to not just be read by anarchists; I wanted it to be read by kids in seventh grade. It was a story that seventh graders, or high school kids, could read and they

could relate to and also discover that there are different ways
to look at the world. One that doesn't involve trying to become powerful, getting stuff or showing off.

I always liked that quote by Woodie Guthrie—the one that
starts off saying, "I hate a song that makes you think you are
no good." Since most Americans don't read, "popular stories"
are usually in the form of scripts which become movies. These
movies, unfortunately, only show the beautiful, the rich, the
ones who make it all seem so easy. They fall in love and when
they do, they do it so damn perfectly. So whenever you watch
it you think—I'm too old, I'm too fat, I'm too stupid, why
can't I get a better job? Why can't my hair look like that? Why
doesn't he love me? And so on. I think it's worse for womyn
but that's another issue entirely. So anyway, I guess I always
strove to write stories that prove to all us poor slobs, us regular folks, that this is our world and we don't need to take any
crap. Yes, this world is tough but there's something within us
all which can bring about positive change.

Margaret: *So we can create our own cultural ideas?*

Carissa: I think that a lot of the writing I've done has focused
on portraying womyn in different ways, allowing them to have
different characters at different ages, doing work that is usually
ignored in Hollywood movies. Because whatever gender you
are, when you watch movies, or read books, you want to like
some characters. You want some people to admire. A lot of
times you basically build your identity around a lot of these images you see and quite simply, most of the time the womyn will
pick female characters to emulate and the men will pick male
characters to emulate. And maybe in that way, fiction has a
lot of influence, because essentially you can create these characters that people can emulate and relationships they should
strive for. You can change who is admired and who is not.

Margaret: *I think that one of the things that* Yours for the Revolution *really has to offer to the anarchist culture that reads it is the critique of gender power dynamics in the punk scene. When I came into punk culture after being politicized, I got the impression that it had started to become a more important thing to understand gender dynamics than it had been in the past?*

Carissa: Before riotgrrl, the punk scene was really bad. It depended on what city you were in though, because a lot of cities were worse than others. I think a lot of the East Coast cities were better. But in the Midwest, all of the boys were in punk bands, and the girls were kinda pushed away from that and put into a groupie position. They weren't being treated very well. And I used to write in my zines that as a subculture, we were striving towards an ideal and this situation surely wasn't ideal, yet true discussion was silenced. I look back on that time and I wonder why I even wanted to be part of "the scene" in the first place. But what were the other options? I mean, mainstream society was not much different.

Fiction has a lot of influence, because you can create these characters that people can emulate and relationships they should strive for. You can change who is admired and who is not.

Margaret: *I think that a lot of the zines and books like yours were really critical in starting to change that attitude.*

Carissa: Yeah, there's nothing like a bunch of people being pissed off. And essentially, womyn had finally had it. The riotgrrls were just so angry. You should have heard the way that the male punks talked about them, in the most degrading, hateful way. "How dare they say these things, they're all so unreasonable..." But when you've been degraded like that, and put into a position where you couldn't be an active member of the scene, even though you knew just as much about music and you had just as much potential to be talented, to have charisma, to have something to say... it makes you pissed off, you know?

So whatever. So what if riotgrrl said that men couldn't take the pictures at Bikini Kill shows and the womyn could? They were pissed off. That's how it works. When people are treated badly for a certain amount of time, and they have to hold it in? It accumulates, and it isn't pretty afterwards. You just have to deal with that. Otherwise, behave better. It's not complicated.

Margaret: *Earlier, you were talking about how it would be nice to reach high school, junior high kids. Do you think that you were able to?*

Carissa: I don't know. Scott has told me that a lot of young kids have come up and told him that the book is their favorite book. But I can't enter the minds of other people. I have no idea what influence it has had. There are some people that liked it. Though if you search my name online, there are a bunch of bad reviews, too, so other people really hated it. It may have touched a nerve for some people.

Margaret: *What do you think about having published with a record label and having self-published?*

Carissa: The book that I'm working on, it will probably be indie published again, because I don't spend my time in the writer's world, where you have the connections to get a big publisher to publish it. I don't want to spend my time there. I'd rather spend my time in the trenches. That's much more interesting to me. I don't want to quit my day job.

Margaret: *There might not be too many authors who don't want to quit their day jobs...*

Carissa: I think the ideal artist is somebody who deals with day-to-day events. And I think that a lot of times they're going to have a lot more genuine and interesting things to say when they're immersed in the world instead of cutting themselves off from it. And in order to really get yourself into those writer communities, you kinda have to cut yourself off from the world because you have to spend so much time on it.

Margaret: So, we should avoid an insular writer culture, with people writing about writers all the time... oh my god, that's what I'm doing with this book. Fuck. I just talked myself into...

Carissa: That's why you gotta hang out in dive bars, you know, take the bus more. You gotta surround yourself with people. You gotta do activism, not just political activism, but also work with community groups on community projects that need to happen, like building a community land trust to increase affordable housing or creating time dollar systems in your communities. That also involves a very anarchist notion of the redistribution of wealth and of collectively running land.

Margaret: I think a couple of my friends just stayed at this place in St. Louis that you were talking about. They had entertaining stories about neighborhood kids coming and demanding that the place be opened, and when it didn't get opened on time, they would spraypaint, "fuck you, so-and-so," on the wall.

Carissa: Yeah, and then they figured out how to break into the building. They learned how to pick locks from people in the neighborhood, but they didn't hurt anything. They would just go in and play office. When they were caught they said, "But we cleaned up afterwards." Ⓐ

"Most people look at a piece of technology and ask, 'What does that do?' and a hacker looks at the same piece of technology and says, 'What can I do with it?'"

—Rick Dakan

RICK DAKAN

Rick Dakan is an anarchist geek. A few years back he was fired from a video game company he helped found, Cryptic Studios (who make the City of Heroes *MMORPG), and soon turned that tale into* Geek Mafia, *a crazy revenge-fantasy crime novel with hacker con-artists as the heroes who scam money from the right-wing. Very enjoyable reading, let me tell you.*

I read through the first two Geek Mafia *books, and then had the chance to read the then-unpublished third book,* Geek Mafia: Black Hat Blues, *which introduces anarchist politics more directly. It was also the first novel I read entirely on a screen, but it was engaging enough to hold my attention.*

I called him and we talked about hackers, role-playing games, publishing, and of course about anarchy.

Margaret: *So you do a good job making your characters' politics a part of their motivations without actually preaching directly to the audience...*

Rick: When you're telling any kind of story, the character in the story has to come first. Anytime it doesn't, the odds are you're going to end up writing a crappy story. It's like hiding vitamins in ice cream.

You want to try to work your politics into it, but only when it naturally fits into the story and the characters. The characters in the story have to come first, always. In every one of my books, there is plenty of stuff about the issues that were raised in each of the books that didn't make it into the novel because there wasn't a place for it; there wasn't a reason for anybody to be talking about it or there wasn't a way that it affected the plot or the story. My primary goal is to tell entertaining stories, and if I can sneak in as much of my worldview as I can, that's all the better.

Margaret: *That gets into what I wanted to ask next: what do you think we can accomplish by writing fiction?*

Rick: I grew up reading mostly science fiction and fantasy, but when it came to start writing my own stuff, it almost all tends to be grounded a lot in the real world, although some aspect of the real world that maybe a lot of people aren't familiar with. It's heightened reality, and some of it is verging towards science fiction. But to more directly answer your question, I think you can portray worlds and ideas and ways of behavior and ways of acting that your reader might not otherwise be familiar with. You open a window into another way of existing, another way of thinking. I think that's what fiction has to give with regards to presenting a political message.

To me, the ideal example, the book that has the highest political content that I agree with that still works tremendously as a book is Ursula K. Le Guin's *The Dispossessed*. She gives this compelling, thought-out vision of an anarchist society, but it's a story first. It's a novel about relationships and people; when I gave it to my mother, who is your basic middle-left middle-class American democrat, unfamiliar with any of the politics, she could just enjoy it and love it as a great story. And it opened up the idea, "Oh, so this is how a world like that might work."

So this is what the role of fiction is. It's almost like presenting models, like a concept car. Like how the auto industry puts out all these crazy cars that they never expect to build, but it gets people to think about some particular aspect of car design.

The other thing is that you just never know. You want to put out a book that is genuine and feels true, that conjures up thoughts and images that you want people to have, and you just never have any idea how someone is going to run with that. It could have a big effect. I have friends who grew up in dysfunctional households without a lot of reliable guidance and got their moral core from Dragonlance *Dungeons & Dragons* novels. That's a true story, that's where that guy, as a kid, got a sort of a moral compass. And that's because [authors] Margaret [Weis] and Tracy [Hickman] put that in there. I used to know Tracy Hickman fairly well, and he's a great guy and we get along well—our beliefs are very different, he's a Mormon— but he's expressing that sort of core morality in his stories. I don't know that he ever intended for his fantasy novels to be a moral compass for some kid in Philadelphia, but it happens.

You want to try to work your politics into it, but only when it naturally fits into the story and the characters. The characters in the story have to come first, always.

Margaret: *That's interesting, the idea that you put things out in the unknown and people will react to them however they'll react to them.*

Rick: Exactly. Your only real job is to throw that mirrored ball out there and hope it reflects the things you want reflected.

Margaret: *How did you get into anarchism?*

Rick: I think that the first thing that came across my plate was *The Temporary Autonomous Zone* by Hakim Bey, and I don't even know where the hell I got a copy of that. That sort of got me rolling. And *The Dispossessed*, that would be the first explicitly anarchist text that I really engaged with that made it make sense to me.

I'm trying to remember how I came across AK Press, because almost immediately after I came across AK I became a Friend of AK, where I contribute 20 bucks a month or whatever and they send me everything they put out. I was doing that before I had met any of those guys. I met Ramsey [the founder of AK Press] at Book Expo America in 2006 and I'd already put out *Geek Mafia* myself at that point.

> You can portray worlds and ideas and ways of behavior and ways of acting that your reader might not otherwise be familiar with. You open a window into another way of existing, another way of thinking.

Oh! I can't believe I forgot this, because I've been out of comics for so long. It was Grant Morrison, it was *The Invisibles*. That got me to the Hakim Bey, from Grant Morrison's site, and it went from there. I was reading a lot of comics while I was doing "The City of Heroes," that superhero videogame, but I ended up reading a lot of non-superhero comic books, like *The Invisibles, Transmetropolitan, Sandman.*

Margaret: *How about writing? How did you get into writing?*

Rick: I was an undergraduate back in the early nineties for history, and I'd been a pen-and-paper role-playing game player, *Dungeons & Dragons* and that kind of stuff, since elementary school. When I went off to graduate school, I was in a gaming group and a friend of mine and I were going to a big role-playing game convention in Milwaukee called GenCon. He was a programmer for CompuServe at the time and he knew someone from message boards who had just gotten a job at White Wolf [an RPG publisher] in charge of *Wraith* [a game]. Are you an RPG player?

Margaret: *Yeah, I was just playing* Dungeons & Dragons *last night.*

Rick: Ah! I run a weekly Sunday game. [*And then we geek out about RPGs for several minutes.*] Anyway, *Wraith* was launching that week at GenCon, and on the drive over there we came up with a pitch, and we pitched it and they bought it, so we got the contract to write a gamebook. So while I was in grad school, I started doing that for extra money and then it just took over. So from 1995–2000, I was pretty much doing full-time pen-and-paper RPG design and writing. I worked on 30 different books at that time. That's how I got my start, which was a great way to start because I was making not a lot of money, but enough to do it full-time. And since it was low money and high word count, I developed a good work-from-home ethic and the ability to write a lot—2,000 words a day, 5 or 6 days a week. Which has continued to serve me well. Then I went from that into then having the idea for the computer game, then after that a comic book based on the videogame, and now the novels.

Margaret: *What is it like working with radical publishers verus other kinds?*

Rick: Well, I've worked for Wizards [a major RPG publisher], so that's pretty mainstream. For sure there's a difference. That's when I've had to make the most changes to things. I was doing some Dragonlance stuff, so there were a lot more people with their fingers in the pot about what's appropriate and about whether or not you can have your ogre bathe in a cauldron full of elf blood or not. That was a specific thing that was in there that I had to call back. I've never had to for novels.

This new one, I'm just about to start shopping around to bigger publishers because I kinda need to make more money with it, so we'll see. I do know just from my limited exposure that once you get into that area of experienced dedicated fiction editors, they have a lot of things that they expect and a lot of things that they don't like just out of hand. The great thing about working with PM Press [a radical publisher] has been they just react to the material based on whether or not it works for them rather than, "Does it fit into this box neatly?" or, "Does it follow this format?" If we could sell more, I would never go anywhere else. That's probably true of a lot of writers.

It's so tough these days. We're in an awkward stage, though I think it's actually going to get better for creators. With *Geek Mafia*, when I put it out, I had a distribution deal, and they got it in front of the book buyers for the two chains, for Barnes & Nobles and Borders. And it's just one person who makes that decision. Your book has that one shot at that one meeting and that's whether or not it gets ordered for the whole country. Borders actually picked it up and carried it, but didn't order many, in a phase when they were experimenting, so they were taking more stuff but they were returning it 60 days later if it didn't catch. So it was like, "Oh wow, Borders ordered a bunch," and then, "Oh, Borders sent them all back." So that's gonna get better as it gets easier to reach directly to people, as it's already getting better for musicians. I read most of my books on my Kindle [an eBook reader] these days, and print-on-demand and all of that kind of stuff will help. But we're at an awkward phase with media right now.

Margaret: *Since I started doing these interviews about two years ago, the publishing industry has been shattered; it's changed drastically. You're in a good position to be watching it from the point of view of someone who is both radical but also wants to make your living through writing.*

Rick: Everything is even more complicated given recent economic events. Everything is cracking up. Everything is niche-ifying. The big publishers are getting more skittish. The big document for me of the last year or so was Kevin Kelly's blogpost "1,000 True Fans." His point is, and he does the math on it, if you, as a creator, can get 1,000 true fans—and a true fan is defined as someone will over the course of one year will spend one day's wages on products you produce—then that's all you need. If you could have 365 days of someone's average wages, that should be all you need. And 1,000 true fans come with 5,000 casual fans and 10,000 one-time fans. And so I think that's the way to go, but it's just getting over that hump. For me, ideally, I'd sell *I, Avatar* [Dakan's upcoming novel] to a publisher that would put enough muscle behind it that I could get enough eyeballs that I could capture. And then I'd go back to doing it myself or doing it through PM. It's just finding that audience.

I've learned the lessons of times when I could have been more focused on capturing and retaining the audience that I've had and squandered those opportunities that I'm now kind of regretting. I think that's the key. I think that to succeed as a writer, or any creator, that element of self-promotion is just gonna get more and more important. The onus is gonna fall on each individual to create their own world, which I think is great, I think that's absolutely the way it should be. It's just a matter of doing it, which can be a pain, and not everyone is gonna succeed. I'm certainly happier to have a world with 100 people who sell 5,000 books as compared to 5 people who sell 100,000 books. I think that's a much more interesting world to be in.

I really do see it all coming down. Maybe not in the next 5 years, but maybe the next 15. Have you played with a Kindle at all?

Margaret: *No, not yet. I've still got this thing for dead tree books, too.*

Rick: Yeah, a book is a great piece of technology, there's no denying it.

I had some eBook reader that I really liked but I stopped being able to use it when I switched my computer over to Linux. But the new Kindle, the screen is a lot easier to read. They're still too pricey to catch on mass-wise, but when they're $75 in a few years? The built in wireless, books just appear on it that I pre-order, plus it can hold multiple books at once. And for whatever reason, I actually find that I read faster and easier on it. I think that that kind of technology, whatever form it takes in the next 5 to 10 years is going to heighten the ability for authors to circumvent the publishers and the stores and go directly to the people.

But then it will be all about how do you actually reach the people, and who are the tastemakers, and that will be a whole new set of challenges. Those tastemakers are going to become so important. It will be interesting to see. With *Geek Mafia*, I met Cory Doctorow at a hacker con, and gave him a copy and he liked it, and he said he was going to write a nice review. I said, "Okay, I'll set up a sale on my website before you post the review," and so he posted the review and a link and I sold like 600 books in 18 hours.

Margaret: *Yeah, he did the same thing to me.* SteamPunk Magazine *got BoingBoing'd and it changed my life from casual zinemaker who found odd jobs to publisher.*

Rick: Those people like him are going to become even more important figures. That's what my next novel that I'm going to be starting in a couple months is going to be about, among many other things. I think that's really fascinating. And I have no idea where that's going to go, how that's going to work. Clearly, media companies are going to try to co-opt that as much as they can.

Margaret: *Your work deals a lot with the human side of technology, and it's nice to see stuff coming from radicals about* *how technology can be liberating, and how it can be used to get over on The Man. You come at this from a hacker point of view, so I'm curious what you think about the liberating aspects of technology.*

Rick: I think they're just tremendous. You've hit on one of my pet peeves, you see it in radical circles and you see it in writer circles—specifically literary and poetry circles—that sort of automatic distaste for technology and the fetishization of nature. I find that nature and technology, they're all one spectrum of things. My definition of a hacker, most people look at a piece of technology and ask, "What does that do?" and a hacker looks at the same piece of technology and says, "What can I do with it?" And that's the key thing that I like to highlight. For the most part, most technology is morally neutral. There's weaponry and toxins and things like that that maybe aren't, but I see technology in general as what you make of it. I think that it's important to try to think about making good of it, because you just can't ignore it. That's just not going to work. And there are a lot of benefits to not ignoring it.

To succeed as a writer, or any creator, that element of self-promotion is just gonna get more and more important.

Margaret: *I like your definition of a hacker a lot.*

Rick: Yeah, feel free to run with it. I've seen people use it in talks in hacker cons. That sort of catches what I love about hacker culture, that ethos of exploration and re-purposing and finding out how things work, it's a great community. I wish that it were more political here in the US. There's a really deep divide in the US between the political hacking scene and the absolutely not-political hacking scene, which you don't find in, say, Germany where they're pretty much all very radical. Or they just don't care about politics, but their natural assumptions are very radical.

There's a lot of great energy in that, but I guess the hacker community cuts across all political spectrums, and it's got a fairly high libertarian quotient. American libertarianism I find tiresome, and sort of morally and intellectually bankrupt. It just drives me nuts. But it's easy—it's easy for a middle-class technology worker to just say that they're a libertarian, and that gives them an excuse to not think about the issues.

Like I said, there's a lot of creative and interesting energy in the hacking scene but it's all over the place. And part of it is that a lot of them are in the security business.

Margaret: *I'd picked up on that specific quote of Sacco's [an anarchist hacker character] in* Geek Mafia #3, *that European hackers are more into politics than US hackers as a whole. Then Sacco goes on to point out that eschewing politics entirely is bullshit. And it seems like that's what a lot of authors do, eschew politics entirely. Not that everyone has to have the same politics as me, but people just pretend it doesn't exist.*

We're starting out from the premise that not everyone is going to read the book. So just do a book that is honest and you can't be worried about who you're going to offend. Especially, you shouldn't worry about offending people you find offensive. They're the last people that I'm worried about offending.

Rick: Yeah, I find that just so strange. I got a review from a person on a blog who really hated *Geek Mafia*—which is fine, there are plenty of people who hate things that I love and love things that I hate—but his biggest complaint was that I put my politics into it instead of just telling the story. But there is no story without the politics in it. If people don't want to talk about it, that's their prerogative, and I'm definitely not the kind of person who says, "You should do this with your art," but if it's something that you care about, I'm not going to say that you *should* do this with your art, but I *am* going to say you shouldn't *be afraid* to do it with your art. So, for example, I had readers of early drafts say, "You're going to offend some Republicans with this and that's costing you readers." But you know, we're starting out from the premise that not everyone is going to read the book. So just do a book that is honest and you can't be worried about who you're going to offend. Especially, you shouldn't worry about offending people you find offensive. They're the *last* people that I'm worried about offending.

I've had people who liked the book who didn't like the political parts of it, but there are readers out there who can separate the two. I'd like to see more authors put their politics into their work, but at the same time I don't want to see more *Atlas Shrugged*s out there. For all kinds of reasons I don't want to see more *Atlas Shrugged*s out there. It's just not a good book. On one level it's an evil book, but it's also just not a well-written story.

Margaret: *How has the tech scene reacted to your books?*

Rick: I get very positive receptions at hacker cons and things like that. A few weeks from now, *Black Hat Blues* is coming out, and it's the one most directly on hacker culture. I spent much of 2006 going to hacker conventions, so a lot of the stories in the first third of that book are fictionalized versions of things that really happened.

It takes place at ShmooCon, which is a real convention. My friend Heidi who runs it makes an appearance in the novel. She says she read it with her hand over her face, peering through her fingers. She was enjoying it, but at the same time she was like, "Oh god, I know who that is..." It will be interesting to see what the reaction from the hacker cons will be now. I think it will be good, because it's made up but it's all true. I tried to portray the community in a relatively nuanced, true way.

Margaret: *How about from the anarchist scene, or the radical scene?*

Rick: Not as good, certainly. First of all, they just don't read fiction. I went to the San Francisco anarchist bookfair. And I had the only new novel there. New York too. When I was behind the table, you'd just get a confused look from people, "It's a novel?" I don't know; it seems like a tougher nut to crack. It's funny, because I got an interesting review, from some lefty website or magazine, who hated *Geek Mafia: Mile Zero*. The thing that he was upset about was that basically, it was like he was Winston [a traditionally radical character]. Everything I critiqued about Winston, about the reactionary old guard? Clearly he was just that guy. So I was actually pleased with that negative review. It was pretty savage, but it seemed like I managed to hit the nail on the head.

As much as I love most things about anarchism, we make Democrats look like the most unified people in the world. The splintering within the anarchist scene is a thing to behold. I haven't gotten enough feedback to know for certain, but you almost run the risk of offending more people cause there're more little ways to offend people. But who knows? Maybe they'll just be happy to have the scene portrayed in some sort of positive light.

Margaret: *So the radical scene is often confused when they're presented with fiction. One of the things that I'm trying to promote with this book is that it's okay to write fiction, and that it's okay to write fiction that isn't just a dry, non-story description of a utopia. Do you have any ideas?*

Rick: I don't have any silver bullet ideas, but I think the only way to change a culture like that is to keep throwing options at them. There's that standard marketing truism, that a person sees a product seven times before they decide to buy it. You might be able to extrapolate from that that they just need to be presented with the idea that there's fiction out there for them and that hopefully that'll seep into their understanding of their options for entertainment. It's interesting, what is that American libertarianism I find tiresome, and sort of morally and intellectually bankrupt. It just drives me nuts. But it's easy—it's easy for a middle-class technology worker to just say that they're a libertarian, and that gives them an excuse to not think about the issues. culture's reading habits, their entertainment habits? I don't know that I know enough about that. It's one of those things where you go into it thinking that everyone thinks like you, but then you're there and I just don't actually understand, as it turns out. And I don't have a whole lot of time to try to understand, you know? That's part of my difficulty with having such disparate reading groups. Who do I talk to, who do I reach out to? It's easy to do a little for everybody and not enough for anyone.

I'd be really interested in hearing what you find out, because it's a nut worth cracking. There's a lot of value there. For a lot of reasons. Maybe people take themselves a little less seriously when they're dealing with fiction, which I think is usually a good thing, and it's also a good way for people to reach out, like *The Dispossessed*. Or with my stuff, like, "Hey, here's this book you can give to a friend or a loved one or to your local library. Here's some of our ideas, enjoy." See what happens. Ⓐ

"There're benefits to books having cultural power, but there's that power thing again. Power attracts types sometimes that are more attracted to the power than the actual passion for the actual medium."

—Jim Munroe

JIM MUNROE

Jim Munroe is a writer of all sorts of things. He's written novels, such as Everyone in Silico *and* Flyboy Action Figure Comes with Gasmask. *He's written comic books, like the post-rapture* Therefore Repent! *and* Time Management for Anarchists. *He writes videogames and movies. He self-publishes near-everything he does, and he runs a website,* NOMEDIAKINGS.ORG, *which holds an extensive collection of DIY articles to help other people do the same. His publishing label, No Media Kings, is an open one, which he invites other people to brand their work with.*

He's also pulled some interesting activist stunts using his skills as a writer, some of which he told me about when I called him in Canada. We also spoke about different mediums, anarchism, PR, and how to derail art back into the cultural gutter where perhaps it belongs.

Margaret: *So you're a big fan of self-publishing, or at least alternatives to mainstream publishing. Why is that?*

Jim: I think one of the best ways to oppose media consolidation is by proliferation of small, independent presses and media outlets of all sorts. One way is to directly critique and confront consolidation in all its forms; if that's tearing down, then building up is working on building viable, sustainable alternatives to it.

Margaret: *You encourage other people to make things as well, to write stories. Is this to try to break down the pedestal that authors are on?*

Jim: For sure. My feelings about other creators is that they aren't competitors. A lot of people are caught in this mindset that somehow other people making stuff is going to take food out of their mouths. And that's never made any emotional or rational sense to me. Basically, what I've gotten from what other people create is just as valuable as money that I would get from someone who bought a book. That's just as sustaining to me as money to pay rent or to buy food.

Margaret: *So a mutual aid situation, instead of a competitive one?*

Jim: Yeah. The whole zero-sum game mentality has never made any sense to me, because the majority of my formative creative time was in a community, specifically in the zine community. I also went to university for creative writing, got a BA in creative writing and English, and in university there was more of a sense of, "Only one of you will be a published author." But I was kinda immune to that because it was being proven wrong by my life experience.

Margaret: *How did you end up making the move from just doing zines to work in lots of different mediums, like books and interactive fiction?*

Jim: Part of me was intrigued by doing a book with a spine instead of in a saddle-stitch format, but really there're lots of zines that are better quality and more interesting than books. I'm an unrepentant medium-hopper. I enjoy many different mediums, and it makes sense for me to want to do stuff in lots of different mediums. I'm lucky enough that I'm connected to a community of makers, many of whom have different skills in terms of art, or directing, different kinds of skillsets, so the possibility of collaborating with people who are very talented in those areas is really appealing.

I think one of the reasons that working in different mediums is fun for me is that I enjoy transgressing boundaries, which probably relates to my anarchist tendencies. A lot of people, when faced with the idea of having to going over a boundary, such as going from novelist to filmmaker, or from novelist to computer-game maker, they find that intimidating, it makes them uncomfortable. Even though it's largely a fictional or socially invented role, people are more comfortable within those roles than transgressing them. And I get a kick out of that. I get energy from things that other people find draining.

Margaret: *What do you think can be accomplished by writing fiction?*

Jim: One of the reasons I write science fiction in particular is that when people believe in something that is stated from the outset to be fantastical, they're opening themselves up to new possibilities.

My feelings about other creators is that they aren't competitors. A lot of people are caught in this mindset that somehow other people making stuff is going to take food out of their mouths. And that's never made any emotional or rational sense to me.

I feel like that's a muscle that, the more we exercise, the more potential we have for really thinking about creative solutions about our real life. I like writing science fiction as well because people assume it's a trash, or a cultural-gutter kind of genre. I enjoy crafting what I consider to be good writing within that genre because people read it and they have to reassess their beliefs. "Well okay, I don't like science fiction, but I like your work," is something I hear a lot. And that's great, because it means that I've overturned someone's assumptions about what is low and what is high art, about what they like and what they don't like. If they question that, they're more likely to question other things in their daily lives. I think fiction in general has a potential to get people into a more creative line of thinking about real life as well.

Margaret: *Can you tell me the story about how you and some people set out to fight gentrification with science fiction stories as graffiti?*

Jim: Sure. It started with a little talk I gave at Active Resistance [a radical conference] in 1998. I had a talk about grafting activism and science fiction together as a radical, creative beast that could hopefully transform society. I called it Science Friction or something like that. What we decided to do was to address the gentrification that was going on in Kensington Market [a neighborhood of Toronto]. We wrote Kensington Market 2020 stories; one-page stories that brought to light some of the possibilities for the future of the neighborhood. We made photocopies and put them up as flyposters in the market with a little email address for people who were interested, though largely it was intended as a piece of public art for anyone walking by so they could read about our possible visions of the future of the neighborhood.

That was pretty fun, so we did it again for two other streets, one was addressing consumerism, Queen Street West 2020, and one was addressing the future of education, called U of T 2020, University of Toronto 2020. We did a couple of those flyposter series. It's hard to gauge the success of those types of things, but our intent was engage in the public in a broader way than just at anarchist gatherings.

Margaret: *One thing that I've found interesting is that you have very non-traditional PR when you put a book. You used to be an editor for* Adbusters, *so you clearly choose carefully where you advertise your books...*

Jim: Yeah, I have a sensitivity to stupid advertising, which is what drew me to *Adbusters* in the beginning. As much as I have an aversion to advertising, there is a social value to telling people about cultural products and other products. The problem is that it's so over-emphasized in our society that you get a sort of hype-nausea from an overdose of hype. A little hype isn't so bad, but the amount that we're constantly assaulted with is ridiculous. I had to figure out a way to promote my own work that I felt good about.

My favorite so far was my *Everyone In Silico* campaign. The difference between me doing promotion for my books versus someone else doing it is that I'm far more creatively invested, so it's way more engaging and I'm also kind of creatively closer to it so it actually makes me more effective than an average PR firm that is used to doing whatever for whomever.

It really came together for that particular book. I was just going through the manuscript, and I had had to mention all of these brands because in the future the brand intensification is even more than it is now, but I feel a little silly giving them free advertising in my book. So I actually invoiced them for product placement. Proactively, before they've actually agreed to it or found it interesting or are even aware of it. I liked that idea. It also came from a dissatisfaction from how I'd promoted previous books, where I was just reading a couple sections from them. I felt like that was a broken way to promote them, giving people a taste of a book. It would be like, "Oh I got this new song... Da du-dah.... [*Jim sings a few notes*]." You play a few notes from a novel and you don't really get across the same thing as it would be to be alone with the book sitting on your couch or whatever. That inherent disjointedness of a traditional novel reading, combined with the complete inadequacy of most writers to dramatically perform their readings—which is kinda what's necessary for an engaging performance—leads to fucking trainwreck after trainwreck of reading. So I was dedicated to the idea of working with things that were more performative. I'm not necessarily a very good performer, but even a bad performer is better than an inadequate reader.

Writing those past due letters was fun because it let me take more direct stabs at these companies that I'd mentioned, allowing me to bring up various things I knew about their evil corporate histories that I wasn't able to really discuss in the book. Because one of the things about the future in *Everyone in Silico* is those corporate crimes aren't really known... the futuristic element is that people aren't critical of corporations anymore. It's become such a part of our lives that we can't imagine what it would be like without them. So to maintain the integrity of the book I couldn't take the shots at the corporations that I secretly wanted to. The letters allowed me a forum to make more direct political critiques of the corporations and at the same time create something more suitable for doing a reading.

I feel a little silly giving all these brands free advertising in my book. So I actually invoiced them for product placement. Proactively, before they've actually agreed to it or found it interesting or are even aware of it.

It was a great success in that people really responded in an immediate way and left with a sense of where the book was coming from, rather than a literal translation.

Margaret: *On your website it's mentioned that most radical presses are shying away from fiction as a risky investment. Why do you think that is?*

Jim: Often people who run radical presses, their first passion isn't necessarily fiction. They might like fiction *as well*, but it's kind of specialized in some ways. If you look at the requirements from a publisher for non-fiction versus fiction... for instance, you can sometimes write a non-fiction book and get an advance for an outline, but you can never do that—unless you're incredibly well-established as an author—with a novel. You have to have the novel written essentially and you submit it and hope they go for it. Even with publishers for whom fiction is their bread and butter and it's kind of their main thing, they're more conservative.

There's just an element where people aren't 100% sure of their tastes. They know what they like from non-fiction radical books. They also realize that there's a tremendous amount of work that's required once you do start accepting fiction. Because there's just going to be an onslaught of manuscripts coming in, and that requires some sort of management. If you consider a radical community, how many people would consider sitting down and doing the research and writing a book on Emma Goldman versus the number of people who would write a memoir-style story about their lives? You'd get way more of the latter, and you'd basically have to deal with, regardless of quality, a huge amount of ego and logistical stuff, dealing with the amount of mail you would get and whatnot. Even if you're thinking outside of the radical community, like if you get listed in one of those places like Writer's Market, you just get so much stuff in the mail that it becomes a job unto itself. I think those are some considerations.

Margaret: *How do we encourage radical fiction? It seems like there's a pretty strong disconnect between people interested in theory versus people interested in reading fiction.*

Jim: I would say that there're a lot of creative punks, but there're lots of not-so-creative punks, you know what I mean? I like punk rock in the sense that it... looked at it in one way, it's kinda like a cosplay [costume play, like the people who wear Star Trek uniforms to conventions] situation. Most punk rockers would not find that amusing for instance. [*He says as I laugh.*] I think that the whimsy that comes with fiction is something that is missing from the scene. I mean, there's also a strong element of punk rock that *doesn't* take itself seriously.

But that's where I think the disconnect is, is that people are not so into the humor side of things sometimes. Maybe that's for the best. I think that if punk rock was just this big joke it would lose some of its cultural significance. As I said, I'm torn about it, because I think, "Ah, I wish they could lighten up," but then I realize that they *have* to take it seriously. If they really do feel like there's something wrong and that they want to change it, they have to have a certain determination and bring a certain amount of gravitas to the table. So I feel your pain. It would be cool if there were more people who were into doing it, but I also think that there's plenty of people on the fringes.

The thing that I found really interesting, I did that Time Management for Anarchists seminar at infoshops and, as I said, I'm not the best performer, but there was a, "Are you making fun of us?" kind of vibe. Because I don't wear the uniform and I haven't since I was a teenager, so that was a little bit.... Those were the people I intended the ideas to be for, for people who were younger, frustrated with not being as organized as they would like, to give them a few handy tips to help them fuck shit up.

But what I found, weirdly, was that when I put it online, it found a whole different audience of people who were punk-friendly and punk-interested, but they wouldn't identify as punks or even as anarchists. They were interested in those things, and maybe would be dissatisfied, but wouldn't necessarily be part of the subculture. What I found is that it probably helped way more people, even though I never intended it for that audience. Not to say that I'm not interested in telling stories for the anarchist audience anymore, but it is something that has been interesting to me. When you open it sometimes, it finds an audience of people who maybe need it more and are broader.

Margaret: *I had a similar experience running* SteamPunk Magazine... *I'm so used to writing for the anarchist and zine subcultures, and all of the sudden it was appealing to an incredibly broad internet culture that wasn't necessarily as radical. It confused me at first but I think in the end it was good.*

Jim: That's interesting, because it's a serialized thing, so did you find that you loosened up your writing, or included things that otherwise you wouldn't have, or didn't include things you would have?

Margaret: *Yeah. Because I had this particular version of what steampunk was in my mind, and I found myself realizing that all of these other people had all of these other ideas and that I should actually listen to them as well and write about things, include things I wouldn't have otherwise.*

Jim: That's interesting. I think I found that with humor in particular, it was sort of tolerated but not really encouraged within the anarchist scene. With tons of exceptions of course, but it gets weird when I call something *Time Management for Anarchists* or I use the word anarchism. I think it makes people uncomfortable, like "That's not my anarchism. Don't proliferate your version of anarchism in this whimsical or not-serious or capitalist or whatever way" that they imagine that I'm creating. Which I understand, I don't take it lightly, the use of the word. I wouldn't do the same thing with, say, communism. The only reason I would name something *Time Management for Anarchists* is that I feel like the content of it is such that it draws people more deeply into the idea than if I called it *Anarchism for Anarchists* or something like that. That intentional dissonance is useful as propaganda. Because in the end, I am an anarchist. Even anarchists can get something out of this. I believe in anarchism as a set of a ways of thinking about the world and have for close to 20 years at this point. Even though my nature is to subvert and make fun of everything, in this case I feel like it's in the service of exposing more people to the ideas. Because I think in the end they are useful ideas.

I don't think like, "Oh you should be exposed to these ideas because I want you to be like me." But it's rather like, "Actually, that constant dissatisfaction that you have at your job might be totally normal for you and it's not something that you should be constantly be ashamed of or be fighting. In fact you should harness that to do what *you* want." Anarchism has weirdly played this role in my life where it's been normalizing. Where it's sort of said, "Actually, yeah, those feelings that you feel every time you're in a power-charged situation is not cause you're fucked up." Well maybe cause I'm fucked up, but the reason I'm feeling these ways is connected to this philosophy about the corrosive nature of power.

Margaret: *How did you get interested in anarchism?*

Jim: Just hearing about it from reading Crass record labels or Conflict sleeves. When I was about 14 or 15 there was an anarchist ungathering in Toronto, and I had my cool aunt bring me to it. I can't say in particular, "Oh it was really great, that was the gathering that changed my way of thinking." I can't say it was really appealing at first. Punk rock as a scene was way more dynamic and interesting than the discussions that were being had in the sort-of official anarchist ungatherings. The punk rock scene was way more creative, even in terms of the songwriting and the art that went into it.

Anarchism has weirdly played this role in my life where it's been normalizing. Where it's sort of said, "Actually, yeah, those feelings that you feel every time you're in a power-charged situation is not cause you're fucked up."

I did a fair amount of serious reading, George Woodcock's *The Anarchist Reader*, when I was 17. I did my World Issues project on anarchism and did a presentation to my Catholic all-boy high school. That was pretty good; it helped me learn how much I hated being at places like that. In some ways that was more formative than a really artsy, more hippy art school might have been. I became aware of the people that I didn't want to be like. I did a seminar in another class on veganism. I'm still vegan. Around the same time a lot of things were clicking into place politically for me, and since then I've continuingly found them a useful and worthwhile practice.

Margaret: *Do you have any final thoughts on the broad question of this whole book, the intersection of anarchism and fiction?*

Jim: I hope I was coherent enough about the idea of opening people's minds in regards to genre-writing, which is what I do. That's one of the reasons that I'm drawn to video games as well; when it becomes universally accepted that they're either art or a sport or both, depending on who wins the battle, I don't think that I'll be as interested in it as a creator. One of the things that especially draws me to it is that it's got a cultural gutter status. Writing, in some ways, is such a calcified and a socially-sanctioned activity. I almost find it more enjoyable to work in comic books or in games or doing things where the forms themselves are disrespected or are considered culturally low. Because then when I do my best work, I'm not contributing to, "Oh, here's another great piece of writing." There's been lots of those.

I was at the Game Developers Conference last week in San Francisco. And the community around the games scene is quite different from any other that I've ever been in, like the publishing world or even the film world to the small extent that I've been involved with it. In those, there's a real conservativism and a sense of competition that you don't see in games to that extent. And I think that has to do with the fact that everyone is still struggling to figure out what they want to do with it, that the medium is still new enough that there isn't a calcified route to success, or calcified understandings of success. For instance, the idea of self-publishing books still has this vanity-press specter looming over it. When people finish a game and put it online, they're self-publishing it, but no one looks at it that way in the games world. It's just what you do, you put your game online. In their case it's also led to this crazy other kind of success that in some ways it's hard to imagine a similar trajectory in the writing world because it would be such a hard thing to build up your credibility after having self-published. So that's one reason I choose to

> One of the things that especially draws me to videogame writing is that it's got a cultural gutter status. Writing, in some ways, is such a calcified and a socially-sanctioned activity. I almost find it more enjoyable to work in comic books or in games or doing things where the forms themselves are disrespected or are considered culturally low.

self-publish, because I think the more people who do it, the less stigma it will have.

Margaret: *That's the most convincing argument I've ever heard for videogames and videogame writing.*

Jim: In some ways, I can be an advocate for games in a way that when I do it for books or even publishing in general, I feel like I'm just feeding into a very status-quo institution. So there's something that kind of undercuts my enthusiasm for it. I really wasn't aware of it at the time. In some ways, it's kind of interesting. Not to harp on how conservative the publishing industry is, but even in the radical publishing world there's a conservativism that is hard to buck. If you go into it sort of expecting that you'll have a lot more energy for it. But that's why books are given such cultural currency. When you put out a book, it'll be a big deal. Have you put out a book before?

Margaret: *No, I've done a lot zines, but this is my first "book deal."*

Jim: Yeah, you'll feel more legitimate. I certainly did. There're benefits to books having cultural power, but there's that power thing again. Power attracts types sometimes that are more attracted to the power than the actual medium.

Margaret: *I like this thing that you're talking about, how we need to get storytelling out of this conservative niche, and I'm trying to wrap my brain around how to do that. I think that zine culture does a decent job of it, since everyone has a zine it's not such a big deal.*

Jim: I think there's lots of mediums in which storytelling or making art becomes... I don't want to say more inclusive. Let's say less exclusive. Because it creates a sense of artificial scarcity and creates competition amongst people. Because in the publishing world, what gets chosen to get published is a combination of things. It's certainly not the best of the best. Even though that's the way it's presented of course. My theory is that once you're an 80% or better author, in terms of quality, most people can't tell the difference. Maybe some publishers can tell the difference, but generally I think they figure the audience would be just as happy with an 85% book as an 80%. Usually other writers can tell.

But there's a big skew towards people who are good at getting their work out there, that have a story themselves that makes the book easier to sell, because they have a book that has a catchy name or cover, or any of those other things which are fine things unto themselves, but they're not basing it on writing strength alone. I feel like there's a lot of wasted talent. People keep trying to go through the bottleneck of publishers. I actually did an article, "10 ways of getting your writing out there." It's 10 different ways to get stuff out there in ways that are not strictly thinking about books as the ultimate repository of story. When people think, "Oh it's prestigious" and they have it in their heads from an early age that they want to be an author and blah blah blah. But if they know an artist who likes their writing, why wouldn't they collaborate on a comic book?

Movies are an example of something that is actually pretty accessible these days. If you have a story to tell and can take a decent picture, know someone with a DV camera, there's lots you can do to create interesting work that way. In some ways it's way more likely to be watched than to be read. How much more likely am I to watch something that's a 10 minute movie than a 300 page book? I think that people have to assess what their own media habits are, what they're most excited by. Ⓐ

"Stories are how people orient their sense of who they are in the world, and how the world is supposed to be, and how we're supposed to be in it."

—Starhawk

STARHAWK

Starhawk is an activist pagan who has been involved in non-heirarchical organizing for a good deal longer than I've been alive. She's also a fairly prolific writer, writing such non-fiction books as The Spiral Dance, The Earth Path, *and* Webs of Power. *The book that I wanted to talk to her about, though, was* The Fifth Sacred Thing, *a novel that explores two societies: a pacifist-anarchist San Francsisco of consensus organizing, cultural diversity, and mutual aid economics; and a fascistic Los Angeles of rigid hierarchy, racism, and war-mongering.*

I tracked her down when she was speaking at a women's conference in North Carolina, and we spoke about what it means to be a witch and a writer, about what it means to be mildly famous in a culture that eschews fame, about how we can use fiction and storytelling to focus our energies on positive change. And we talked about how to keep our stories from being purely propaganda—that is, how to make sure they stay good stories.

Margaret: *What kind of power can myth and story have? How can storytelling help our activism?*

Starhawk: I think myth and story can have incredible power. They unleash the imagination, and the imagination is where all change begins. You can't make the change unless you can envision it. I think sometimes in our politics we're very good at knowing what we're against, what we're angry about, what we don't want. But we have more power when we have at least some kind of vision of what we *do* want. The nice thing about fiction is that we can create that vision and play it out at very low cost. It's a lot easier to imagine San Francisco transformed than it is to actually go renovate all the buildings. You can do thought experiments.

I think to be good fiction it has to be more than that.... Your characters have to kind of come alive for you. You end up grappling with things that you didn't realize you were going to grapple with when you started out.

I think that stories are how people orient their sense of who they are in the world, and how the world is supposed to be, and how we're supposed to be in it. People use stories to take a look at different ways of being in the world. For me, as a young woman, there were some books that I was tremendously influenced by, in various ways, that were really formative in the process of me telling myself who I am, who I want to be.

Margaret: *What kind of effects do you think that* The Fifth Sacred Thing *has had?*

Starhawk: I think that it's had an effect on people in the movement, in that it's given people a picture of what the world could be like. Many people have said to me, "I want to go live in that place." It's a way of carving out some ground that people can stand on and start thinking, "How do we create the world that we want?"

Part of the political vision that I held when I wrote it was a world that was environmentally balanced, but also a world that was multiracial, multicultural, that was founded on social justice. It was really important that those

> The nice thing about fiction is that we can create that vision and play it out at very low cost. It's a lot easier to imagine San Francisco transformed than it is to actually go renovate all the buildings.

things went together. At the time that I wrote it, approaching 1992 and the 500th anniversary of Columbus, there was a lot of activist work around diversity, a lot of critique of the environmental movement, the feminist movement, and the direct action movement as being basically white movements. We were struggling with these questions of how we could be inclusive. And to me, part of how we can do that is to at *least* be inclusive in your imagination. At least envision a world that very consciously looks at the those questions around race, class, culture, religion, and language, and a society where diversity is seen as a gift.

The other influence that the book had, inadvertently, was around sexuality and polyamory. Which is funny to me now because, for me personally, that's never worked. But when I wrote the book, during a dry period in my life, it was pure fantasy. So I probably inadvertently broke a lot of hearts.

I think that polyamory probably works better for younger people than for people of my generation: for all of our politics and our thinking, we were raised with certain expectations and we're much more constrained than the generations that have come since the sixties and since the gay movement and all of that.

Margaret: *As part of your ecofeminism [in which oppressions such as gender and environmental destruction are viewed as linked], you chose to portray races and genders in a very egalitarian way...*

Starhawk: Because I was writing about a time where people would have in some ways transcended racism, I don't identify people as one race or the other in the book. I try to just describe them. A lot of people never realized that Bird [the protagonist] was black. There are a couple points later in the book where characters actually say something about it as they encounter racism. It was interesting to me that people didn't catch that unless it was labeled.

Margaret: *I notice you did a lot of describing without actually...*

Starhawk: I spent a lot of time on busses and things when I was writing it, staring at people, deep in thought, thinking, "How could I describe that particular shade of skin color."

Margaret: *What kind of place do you think that politics have in fiction?*

Starhawk: For me politics are about engaging the really crucial issues of our times. And I think it's really important to write fiction about that too. I like to write about people who are engaged and passionate, who have a huge desire to do something important like change the world, and what they run up against in trying to do that. Politics are a really fertile ground for writing.

It's very important for us when we do political work to also see our struggles reflected in our culture. And we don't see that all that much. Part of that is because publishers are always looking—especially right now as publishing gets more and more corporate—for what's going to appeal to the mainstream, to the biggest number of people. The life of the activist or the life of an anarchist seems very strange and weird and marginalized and isn't going to sell books. The markets aren't there. The larger culture is not going to reflect the counterculture that we build, but I think it's important for us to have those kinds of reflections, to *create* those kinds of reflections. To use fiction—which is a very powerful tool—for confronting some of those major issues that we confront.

Margaret: *So mainstream publishers are more and more shying away from political fiction, but I've also discovered that a lot of radical publishers shy away from fiction.*

Starhawk: Yeah, you're neither fish nor fowl. Which is probably part of why I haven't written more fiction since *The Fifth Sacred Thing*. Also, for many years I haven't felt like I've had the time and mental space I needed to create a fictional world; I've been too busy doing too many things. It's easier to write non-fiction, because you can say, "Alright, I'll just sit down and write this," whereas with fiction you have to let it grow and evolve.

I think that political publishers are focused on serious, real things. I also think that it's challenging to be writing fiction when you're part of your movement, because you feel accountable to that movement. Because fiction has to involve conflict, it can't just be propaganda. If you're writing fiction, you're grappling with questions that you don't know the answers to. And when you're doing political work, we're usually very clear that we *do* know what the right answers are and everyone should listen to us and follow us. So it's tricky to write fiction that works for your political community but still goes deeper than whatever the particular answers are that we have at the moment.

Fiction has to involve conflict, it can't just be propaganda. If you're writing fiction, you're grappling with questions that you don't know the answers to.

Margaret: *I like that idea, that fiction makes people question, and that maybe it's a better way to get people to question ideology in general? It seems like that's one of the roles of an anarchist anyway, is not to get people to listen to them but to get people to question.*

Starhawk: Writing *The Fifth Sacred Thing*, there were two questions that I was grappling with. One was, I was doing all this research on these peaceful, egalitarian goddess cultures that got overrun and changed into patriarchal cultures. So if you have a peaceful society, how do you defend it against violence? And the other is a question about violence and non-violence. At the time I wrote it I was much more deeply involved in a much stricter form of non-violence than we've seen in the last 10 years or so. But also, being involved in Latin American solidarity work... how do you do non-violence if you're really facing a ruthless enemy? How might it work?

Some people think that the novel is a great novel about non-violence. But in a way it really isn't. Although Tom Hayden [an activist] said that I should have made stronger arguments for violence. But in the end, the success comes when the army rebels and there's violence. It's brought about by non-violence, but I couldn't even in fiction just make it work where the general and the people controlling the army just change their hearts. I mean, I could have just written it, but it wouldn't have made good fiction.

In fiction you need conflict. In life you *get* conflict, but you don't necessarily *need* to have it. Garrison Keillor [a radio personality and author] has a quote, "Things that are horrible for most people are good for writers." I've often thought about that.

Margaret: That's what I always tell myself, if I end up going to jail, plenty of time to write. Still don't want to. Would rather write in the safety of a punk house somewhere.

Starhawk: Sometimes you can get pen and paper, but it's hard to get your laptop in.

Margaret: I spent a little while in The Netherlands, and this person was convicted of throwing a molotov at a cop... she

didn't do it. But she was convicted and only got seven months,
which blew my mind. When she got out, she was complaining,
"They let me have my guitar, but I didn't get my typewriter
until right before I got out."

Starhawk: Yet we've got those two kids from Austin who got
six years for *thinking* about throwing a molotov cocktail.

Margaret: *I interviewed Alan Moore and he had a lot of things*
to say about anarchism and magic, and he was saying that
people usually think about communism and capitalism are
the two poles of political thought, but he thinks that anarchism
and fascism are more useful. He also compares that to magic
and religion, as two equivalent poles.

Starhawk: Well, clearly, I'm deeply involved in magic.
Although for me, I think of magic as being the technology
and the spirituality as being earth-based spirituality, as
being goddess-based spirituality. Although when I got
involved in the seventies, the most important aspect was
that of the goddess being the female image of divinity, the
image of beneficent female power, because it was a counter
to everything I'd grown up with. Now, over the years, I feel
like it's more important to see the goddess as Gaia, the living
planet that we're all a part of, the earth-based aspect of it that
is inclusive of man and woman, and is nature-based. I think
there is an inherit anti-authoritarianism in those traditions,
in spirituality. In any tradition that says you need to locate
spiritual authority in yourself, not in somebody else, not in
some outside force, not in your dead relatives, but within.
I think that it's an important aspect of any kind of anti-
authoritarian political tradition.

I think that roughly I'd agree with him. Capitalism and
communism share a lot. Communism was a kind of odd

hybrid of this egalitarian view of economics that got welded to this top-down view of control. And capitalism is this odd hybrid of this less-controlled view of economics but one that is based on this view of human nature that says that greed is the core of human nature, welded to systems of much more subtle control. And anarchism, in its sort of pure form, is about saying that we want to have societies that are not based on coercive power, but that are based on free association and mutual aid. And we believe that people have a deep desire to make a contribution to society and don't need to be forced to do it, that that's a powerful human drive. We believe in less control and more liberty and freedom. It is opposed to that fascism that creeps into both communism and capitalism that says we must control everything.

At the same time, if you were to ask me what actual practical political policies do I support at this moment in time, I'm probably actually more of a progressive democrat. Go Obama, we need more regulation, we need more government actually providing for human needs and human services, we actually need big structures to do some of the big things that need to be done about climate change while we're evolving to that point of freedom and mutual aid.

Margaret: *I've been running across authors that identify with philosophical anarchism, with anarchism as a desired end result, but think that revolution isn't necessarily the way to get there. I suppose that's how I would presume to identify you?*

Starhawk: Yeah, I'd say at this moment, probably. Maybe it's because in my own lifetime, over the last 40 or more years of being consciously political, having gone through the sixties, believing in the revolution, I don't actually see it happening anytime soon. I don't see most people in the world clamoring for it, and I see a need for some big things to be done that can only be done by big structures.

But I also see an interesting evolution towards non-hierarchical organization. The book that I'm working on now is a non-fiction book on group process and group dynamics in non-hierarchical groups, because I see so many of them struggling over conflict and process stuff. So I decided I should do some research. Sure, I've done 40 years of research on this, but I figured I should at least read what other people are saying about it. And it's interesting, because where you find theory about group behavior and dynamics is either in new-age self-help and pop psychology or in business management. So I've been reading a lot of books from different points of view. And I've discovered this whole series of books that are mostly about the internet. One's called *The Starfish and the Spider* [by Ori Brafman and Rod Beckstrom], which is a very interesting book for an anarchist to read because it's about how organizations are either like a spider, where if you cut off its head the organization doesn't function, or a starfish, which grows a new limb or a new starfish. It's talking about decentralized organizations. Mostly it talks about these things in the context of the internet, about self-organized systems like Wikipedia. Or things like open-sourced software, things that people have contributed to without getting monetary reward because they want to make something happen without anyone organizing it or orchestrating it. It's fascinating to me because I'd never really seen the internet in those terms. But there's this whole other force pushing towards horizontal, non-hierarchical organization that isn't coming from political ideology, or really *any* ideology, but from people's attraction to doing cool things.

Anarchism, in its sort of pure form, is about saying that we want to have societies that are not based on coercive power, but that are based on free association and mutual aid. And we believe that people have a deep desire to make a contribution to society and don't need to be forced to do it, that that's a powerful human drive.

Margaret: *It's interesting to talk to people from the geek point of view, people who are much more used to seeing the internet from those points of view. Essentially, the idea is that as communication proliferates, the need for top-down authority disappears. That's paired, though, in my mind, to the rather dire need of the earth for a little bit less new technology or at least...*

Starhawk: Less new *stuff*. That's one reason I wanted to write a book on group process, because all of those internet books are all gung-ho about how wonderful this all is, and to some degree it is, but few of these people have worked in non-hierarchical organizations for over 30 years or more. And things change over time; new things come up that you can't really anticipate when something is new.

Conflicts come up, and the question of how you resolve conflict when there's no authority in the system is a really interesting one. Because if there's no authority anywhere in a system, there's no way to move a conflict out of a community or resolve it. So it can just sort of reverberate forever until the whole thing is destroyed. And I've see that happen a lot in a lot of collective groups that I've been involved in. They're wonderful for awhile but then when people start grappling with conflict, and people with difficult personalities, they tend to fall apart. They tend to be very short-lived. If by some miracle they become longer-lived, then you get questions like, if everyone has equal say but some people have a much longer-term investment in the organization, is that actually equal? Is that actually fair? How do you work around that? That's what I'm writing about.

Margaret: *You were talking about earth-based spirituality, non-hierarchal spirituality, where the authority is within yourself. I'm under the impression that you're one of the primary people* *who works to carry that over from the spiritual sphere to the political?*

Starhawk: For me, the political sphere and the spiritual sphere or the moral sphere, aren't really separable. And I think that's the core of the philosophy of nonviolence too... you say that you're answering to a higher law, or a deeper law, which means that sometimes you break the law. Martin Luther King had a great definition for an unjust law, which is a law which the people it affects had no voice in making. Sometimes you need to stand in the way of a greater injustice.

I also think that a lot of times people use spirituality as a way to not engage with the political sphere. We have a big ritual in San Francisco every year for Halloween, the spiral dance. Oftentimes, as much as we've brought spirituality into our political activism, we've also brought political imagery into our spirituality. A couple times we've invoked a direction [invoking the four directions is part of many pagan rituals] by... one time we had a bunch of climbers up at the ceiling and when we called in the north, they dropped three giant banners while people were chanting, "Ain't no power like the power of the people cause the power of the people don't stop." We've used political chants that we've done on the streets in the ritual. Sometimes we get feedback like, "I don't come to a ritual to get propagandized."

I've actually written something about how spirituality serves different needs. One of those needs is for comfort, for safety, to provide a community where people feel like they're at home and can lick their wounds. But real spirituality is not just about doing what you're comfortable doing, it's about pushing your edges, about getting pushed into uncomfortable places and grappling with the things that are going on around us in the world as well as the things that are going on within ourselves. I also think that our politics are much more powerful if our political spaces are places where people have room to grapple with the bigger questions, spiritual questions like, "What are we here for," and, "What is life about." I think that those are tremendously political questions. If we don't know what we're here for, then how do we know what we want our society to do for us? If we don't know what we're here for, then how do we counter the point of view that says that we're here to consume products, that we're here to amass as much

Real spirituality is not just about doing what you're comfortable doing, it's about pushing your edges, about getting pushed into uncomfortable places and grappling with the things that are going on around us in the world as well as the things that are going on within ourselves.

physical wealth as possible, that we're here to obey those who are above you in the hierarchy, to give orders to those below you?

Clearly, doing political action isn't easy. People go through really hard things: they get traumatized, beaten and jailed, get attacked, and even sometimes get killed. And you need to have some way to come together to deal with those things. That's where ritual becomes really important, helping us face those things that are too big to face alone.

Margaret: *I want to talk more about story, as it relates to magic.*

Starhawk: In magic we say that manifestation follows the path of energy. And energy follows the path of imagery, and imagery follows the path of intention. So if you're consciously doing magical work, you start with your intention, then find the imagery that reflects your intention, then direct energy through that. That sort of pulls in the force of the manifestation. A lot of the ways we do that, consciously and unconsciously, is through story. We're constantly telling ourselves stories about ourselves and who we are and what we can be. Those stories tend to generate energies. If you're telling yourself stories like, "I'm an anarchist hero fighting the forces of evil," you're going to have a different view of things than if you tell yourself the story that the culture might be telling about you, "You're a loser terrorist about to get stomped by the cops." You create a different emotional energy and probably different actions.

Fiction does that in a more complex way; for it to work you can't just have the positive intention. You have to have an intention countered by a lot of things to create the drama that makes it exciting and makes it a story. The classic story form is you have a protagonist who wants something, has a goal, a desire, and you have something happen to unbalance the status quo and that hero pursues those goals against a series of obstacles, challenges, enemies, until finally there's a resolution.

When I was writing *The Fifth Sacred Thing*, I was thinking about it consciously as magic, that I was creating this vision of the world, and it was like creating a magical image that energy could get poured into. But I also said to myself, "Okay I don't want to create certain parts of that reality."

Margaret: *You don't want to create the fascist society you depicted...*

Starhawk: Yeah, the Bush administration was doing that for us.

But on the other hand, *The Fifth Sacred Thing* had almost this element of prophecy. When I wrote it I could see very clearly two paths of the future, that we had a choice between which one we could go down. So I took each of the them to their logical extreme and said, "What will it be like if they clash?" If they clash we can take a look at them and see them clearly and make choices about them as a culture. I think that that's one of the things that fiction, especially speculative fiction, can do; it can show you those different possibilities and potentials, and it can take you into them at much less cost than actually going there and making those choices yourself to see how they play out. It lets you play them out so that the choices we actually have become a lot clearer. I don't think a lot of people realize that we actually have a choice, that the society that's in San Francisco in *The Fifth Sacred Thing* is actually an option. It gives people a picture of that option, which is a magical act. If we can imagine this, we can do this.

Margaret: *What are the dangers in a non-hierarchal movement of being a storyteller, of having fame?*

Starhawk: It can be a contradiction to be mildly famous in a culture that doesn't believe in fame or celebrity. I don't feel like it's dangerous in the sense that... I don't think that there's any community that would do something just because I said to do it. I think most anarchist community tends to be the opposite. "Starhawk said it so let's not do it, we don't want her to throw her weight around, it'll get too ugly."

Fame is a pain in the ass sometimes, because it gets in the way of just meeting people and having actual connections and relationships with them, but usually that wears off very quickly. It can be more dangerous when... I don't know if it's so much from fiction as from non-fiction, you get a lot of writers and theorists, where people latch onto those theories and take them into action sometimes maybe not because they really had the time or the thought or the experience to work out for themselves what actually makes sense and what's strategic, but because they think that's the way you should do things if you're really an anarchist. You can get people ripe for being manipulated or infiltrated or trapped into doing things.

Margaret: *As soon as you put dogma in the picture, not that we intend to create dogma, but that people could take things as dogma, it really leaves us vulnerable.*

Starhawk: Non-hierarchical things don't work so much through rules as through norms. The thing about norms is that they're often unspoken. They're not overtly imposed, but that makes it even harder to challenge them. I'll give you one example. A couple of years ago I went to the anarchist bookfair, and it was the same day as the Eostar festival, and I was wearing bright emerald green, and it was a complete sea of black. There was not another color among hundreds of people.

It was like a weird psychological experiment. I'd never felt so uncomfortable. It's not like anyone came up to say, "Who the hell are you?" or anything. But it was so powerful. I remember thinking, it's so ironic, here we are, here's the gathering of the people who are the most anti-authoritarian and non-conformist, but there's this total conformity in the color code of what you're supposed to wear. If the anarchist bookfair put something out that said, "You can only enter if you wear black," everyone would be up in arms.

I do tend to wear black a lot, because you can be a witch, an anarchist, or a sophisticated New Yorker with the same wardrobe, all you need to do is switch your accessories. And it's slenderizing and doesn't show dirt. My friend Luisah Teish, she's a Yoruba priest, she's always on my case about wearing black because it attracts all the energies. They always wear white. Part of the

People latch onto those theories and take them into action sometimes maybe not because they really had the time or the thought or the experience to work out for themselves what actually makes sense and what's strategic, but because they think that's the way you should do things if you're really an anarchist.

reason I had them wear white in *The Fifth Sacred Thing* [when the characters decide to "haunt" enemy soldiers] was to try to counter the imagery of black always being negative, white being good, black being death. In the old European traditions, white was the color of death, but black was the color of fertile earth, of the womb, of life.

Margaret: *I was wondering if you had any advice for radical fiction writers?*

Starhawk: When you're writing fiction, you have to serve the story first, rather than serving the politics of the moment. Trust that if you're truly radical, your story is going to actually serve your political ends. And don't be afraid to really grapple with the questions rather than think that you have to put forth the answers.

The other thing I would say is that anarchists don't buy a lot of books. So you might want to think of yourself not just as an anarchist writer but also as a writer who deals with these things. If you're really true to the story, to the human conflicts in the story, they're going to resonate with a larger circle of people than just your anarchist friends. Go out and meet more people outside of that circle, and that will make you a stronger writer.

And to remember Garrison Keillor's quote: "Things that are horrible for most people are good for writers." The advantage of being an anarchist writer is that you often have more life experience than a lot of other people. I've been doing screenwriting, and have a Hollywood agent. And Hollywood is full of all of these kids who get out of school and want to be screenwriters but have no life experience, have never done anything but go to movies and write screenplays. I've met editors who are like that too, they've never *done* anything. They end up somewhere not knowing how to call a taxi to get to the hotel and they're in terror. Being a radical you get a lot of life experience and you get to see a lot of things that other people don't get to see. You get to experience a level of reality that a lot of people don't get to experience. And I think that it's important that we do write about that, that we put that out in ways that can touch people on those deeper emotional levels that fiction can reach. Ⓐ

Conclusions

So what the hell are we going to accomplish by writing fiction? As it turns out, plenty of things. I think that perhaps we anarchists, in our desire for direct action, overlook the beauty and subtlety of the symbolic.

I'm not going to argue that all we need to do is write books or tell stories around the hearth. Of course not.

The other night, I asked my friend—a committed activist—what she thought could be done to stop mountaintop removal mining in Appalachia. "You know what I'm going to say," she said. "We need to completely dismantle the capitalist system." And she was right: even if we enacted laws to protect the mountains, money would find its way around. Even if we blocked every road with our bodies, the state would remove us. Those mountains aren't going to be safe until the entire system is uprooted, and those roots run deep.

But fiction is a part of that uprooting. We need to be inspired and we need to inspire. And fiction offers the chance to explore things deeply in ways that other mediums can't.

What's more, some of us learn more from fiction than theory. This was something I was vaguely ashamed of for a long time, something I kept to myself: I don't much like reading theory. Even stripped of its academic language, it rarely holds my attention. I used to think that made me a worse anarchist or something, but it turns out that I'm not alone.

Fiction is even more important for the young, because we model our ideal selves on role models. We need heroes to learn from, and we need anti-heroes to remember that none of us are, or will ever be, perfect.

And we need to tell stories about ourselves, because others are talking too. Every book and movie out there with a cop as a hero, saving the world from terrorists and thugs hellbent on chaos? We need to counter that. We need books about the oppressed, about the beauty of resistance.

And honestly, we just need stories with some damn teeth. It's hip these days to be apolitical, detached. There are books coming out that aren't afraid of a little meaning, but by and large we're in a sea of cultural vapidity.

Not that we need to see the world one-dimensionally. There's more to life than politics, and not all anarchists are wonderful and not all statists are assholes. But this is one way in which fiction really shines: if you did write a dry utopia, devoid of conflict, it wouldn't make a very good story. Fiction is uniquely suited to propose ideas and then say, "Not that this would be perfect, mind you." While so much of our other work—theory and direct action protest alike—presents answers to the world, fiction presents questions. And our job isn't to convert people to anarchism, it's to get them to ask their own questions, reach their own answers.

Learning how to tell stories is a good way to spend your time. It's something that anyone can practice, that anyone can enjoy. But it's also something that some of us are going to specialize in. And we anarchists and DIY enthusiasts have a lot of advantages in trying our hand as fiction writers. For one thing, printing and distribution are in our control: we've got infoshops and online distribution, shows and events to table at.

For another, we've got a wonderful critique of failure: if you don't fail from time to time, you're not setting your goals high enough.

By and large, we reject intellectual property. We know that all of our stories are influenced by our experiences, that ideas don't just come out from nowhere. So we've less fear of success, less fear of useless, heady, and alienating fame. It's certainly better to be respected as a peer than revered as an icon.

And unlike so many cultures in late capitalism, we're not afraid to be earnest. We're not "too cool" to be unapologetically happy that our friends are doing what they honestly want to do, writing what they truly feel moved to write.

So there's no reason to be afraid to start writing, to start storytelling.

Be proud as an anarchist mythmaker. You're in good company and up to good work. The world needs new stories, better stories. Remember though, the world needs more new gardens and less new stripmalls too, so maybe it's best not to get *too* specialized. Ⓐ

appendix A:
ANARCHIST FICTION WRITERS
(include but are not limited to)

I've compiled short biographies of every anarchist fiction writer I could track down. To a great extent, these are authors who, in their own words, identified as anarchists. I've made a few exceptions for folks like Leo Tolstoy (who shied away from the word owing to its connotations of violence but embraced every core tenant of anarchism). Other authors I researched seemed likely to have been anarchists, but I couldn't find enough evidence to include them. I don't want to misrepresent anybody.

What this list is not is a value judgment. Just because an author doesn't identify with anarchism doesn't make her or his books any less valuable, just as knowing an author is an anarchist doesn't make her or his works any better or really even say whether or not she or he is a good person.

But what this list does reveal is that we're far from alone, us writers who dream of real freedom, of a stateless world. Since the beginning of anarchist thought, there have been storytellers in our midst. Some, like Déjacque, explored utopias. Others, like Mirbeau, wrote nightmares. We have in our midst some of the finest, most respected writers in history, and we have untold numbers of zinesters and fireside yarn-spinners. Pacifists and insurrectionists and everything in between. More than one has taken arms against fascists and secret police. Some publish with mainstream presses, others are fiercely DIY. Many have been exiled or imprisoned for their words alone, for treason or obscenity. There have been anarchist writers from so many different nations and races, and in our ranks are more than a few radical queers and feminists.

This list is the tip of the iceberg. It just represents what I've been able to dredge up personally. We've started a collaborative project to further this research, however, at WWW.ANARCHISTFICTION.NET

I get pretty excited about all of this. But rather than present you with some kind of overview in the form of an essay, I'll just present you with bits about the individuals:

Edward Abbey (1927–1989), the author of the controversial novel *The Monkey Wrench Gang* (which was considered too radical by the mainstream and too sexist by many anarchists), is also the "spiritual father" that inspired Earth First!. He was at least philosophically involved in anarchism in college, editing an anarchist paper and eventually writing his thesis on the topic "Anarchism and the Morality of Violence," in which he declared that a peaceful anarchist society could not be created by the use of violence.

Fabrizio De André (1940–1999), a renowned Italian songwriter, poet, and anarchist, was known for his epic and political music. He translated the works of Leonard Cohen (among others) into Italian, and he wrote a novel, *Un destino ridicolo* (A Ridiculous Fate). He made the island of Sardinia his home, and was once kidnapped and ransomed by Sardinian rebels (terrorists/freedom-fighters, take your pick). After his father—a wealthy industrialist who had once been an anti-fascist partisan—paid his ransom, and the kidnappers were brought to trial, Fabrizio reportedly told the court that the rebels "They were the real prisoners, not I." (Although he did not offer sympathy to the higher-ups in the rebel group, who were wealthy already.)

Rafael Barrett (1876–1910), a Spanish immigrant to Paraguay, was the sort of writer whose works were influential on other people who themselves became more influential. He wrote all types of things, including short stories, but his primary vessel was journalism. He wrote and published a lot, running an anarchist newspaper. One of his more famous pieces was *Lo que son los yerbales*, an account of the conditions on Yerba Mate farms. He was also an outspoken anarchist (very much the sort that preferred the pen to dynamite), and for this he earned contempt and was at one point exiled to Uruguay. In his essay *My Anarchism* (as translated by Paul Sharkey), he begins simply: "The etymology is good enough for me 'Absence of government.' The spirit of authority and the standing of the laws must be destroyed. That says it all."

Hakim Bey (1945–) has written a lot of anarchist theory, most famously *TAZ: The Temporary Autonomous Zone* and he has also written a novel, *The Chronicles of Qamar: Crowstone*. This novel, which I could not track down a copy of, is said to be a story of man-boy love. Hakim Bey is infamous for reportedly encouraging pedophilia. WWW.HERMETIC.COM/BEY

Jens Bjørneboe (1920–1976), once called "the greatest failed novelist of the twentieth century," was a Norwegian novelist, playwright, and anarcho-nihilist. Jens wrote honestly and angrily, a trait that found him convicted of obscenity and resulted in his novel *Without A Stitch* being banned in Norway for a time. Perhaps his strongest allegorical work is his last novel, *The Sharks*. He also wrote anarchist theory, expounding on the idea that anarchism was scientific (contrasting with the dogmatic Marxism) and existed in varying degrees. After a lifetime of controversy and alcohol, he took his own life.

William Blake (1757–1827), poet and author of "Illuminated Manuscripts" (protographic-novels), was an anarchist before the word was coined. He was also both a mystic and completely unrenowned in his time. He attacked organized religion fiercely, and published the heretical *The Marriage of Heaven & Hell*. One interesting quote from that book: "Prisons are built with stones of Law, Brothels with bricks of Religion."

Luther Blissett (1994–) is a collective identity that was begun by Italian anarchists in 1994. The idea is that anyone may call themselves Luther Blissett (a name they took from a famous and still-living footballer). Luther Blissett has since done a large number of extravagant, anti-spectacle media stunts and has collectively written an international bestseller, *Q* (which, like the rest of their work, is freely downloadable). When controversial anarchist Hakim Bey was set to visit Italy, Luther Blissett published a book as if it were written by Hakim Bey, which included, among other things, a speech by Josef Stalin. It met with critical success and quickly sold out. Only later was it revealed the the book was a fake. WWW.LUTHERBLISSETT.NET

Steve Booth (n.d.), the former editor of the UK's *Green Anarchist* magazine, wrote a novel entitled *City-Death*.

Jorge Luis Borges (1899–1986) was one of the most famous spanish-language authors in the world and was often a contender for the Nobel prize for literature, but never received it. Some speculate that this was because of his anarcho-pacifist views. An Argentinean and a world citizen, he is known primarily for his short stories, of which he wrote an innumerable quantity.

Gabriel Boyer (1976–) is a musician, a playwright, a singer, a publisher, a writer, an anarchist, and a wanderer. He and a friend run Mutable Sound, a book publisher and music label, which has released three of his books, including *A Survey of My Failures Thus Far*, a collection of seven books from schizophrenic detective novels to gaming manuals for the creation of the game. He wrote and directed an anarchist musical, *Free-Thinking as Commodity*, while living on an anarchist farm outside Eugene, and he traveled the country practicing bedroom theatre, performing plays in people's bedrooms. WWW.MUTABLESOUND.COM

Braindeadnation are the creators of *The Chronicles of Zomaz: the Anarchist Wizard*, a web-narrative/comic of sorts that includes such memorable characters as Aaron the Vegan Shoplifting Monkey. Freely viewable online. DEEDAH.ORG/ZOMAZ

Octavio Buenaventura (1984–), born in Mexico but living in the Pacific Northwest, is the author of an anarchist novella, *Ever & Anon*. His other activities include fighting riot police in the streets and disseminating anarchist propaganda.

Anthony Burgess (1917–1993) is famous today as the author of *A Clockwork Orange*, but it was only one of his over 30 novels. He said that he deeply regretted how the film adaptation seemed to glorify sexual violence, and how easily people misread that book. He was also an anarchist: "I've never had any money, therefore I've no sympathy for capitalists ... I suppose I end up as an anarchist" (from *Anthony Burgess, a biography* by Roger Lewis, 2002). In his younger life, while serving in the British army, he was often in trouble for defying authority, including being arrested for insulting Spanish fascist Franco. In addition to being a novelist, he was an accomplished literary critic, linguist, composer.

Pino Cacucci (1955–) is an Italian anarchist translator and novelist. He's written essays as well, at the very least for the *Red and Black*, an anarchist journal in Australia. That I'm aware of, only two of his novels are available in English: *Tina Modotti: A Life*, the biography of an Italian actress who becomes a revolutionary; and *Without a Glimmer of Remorse*, a historical novel about the legendary Bonnot Gang of illegalists, inventors of the get-away car.

Chris Carlsson (1957–), a San Francisco activist and anarchist, is probably best known for his non-fiction book *Nowtopia* and for being one of the founders of the bicycle protest movement Critical Mass. He was a founder and longtime editor of *Processed World*, a magazine for dissatisfied office workers that started in 1981. He's also written a novel, *After the Deluge*, exploring an anarchist society in a post-collapse San Francisco. WWW.CHRISCARLSSON.COM

The Catastraphone Orchestra (2006–) might be one of the only bands of musicians that writes fiction together. A collection of chain-smokers, mad scientists, and drug-addled minds, they write in the long-antiquated "seasonal" style of fiction as well as penning manifestos and journalistic forays into the past.

Carolyn Chute (1947–) is a working-class anarchist author who writes primarily about life in rural Maine, where she lives. She's the author of numerous novels, from 1985's critically acclaimed *The Beans of Eypgt, Maine*, to 1999's critically hated *Snow Man*—about a militiaman who kills a senator. She's part of the Second Maine Militia, which is a left-libertarian militia group. There's an interesting interview with her about her radical politics in Eberhardt Press's *No Hope*.

Carissa van den Berk Clark (n.d.), author of *Yours for the Revolution* and *May It Come Quickly Like a Shaft Sundering In the Dark*, is an anarchist and a social worker who came from the punk rock travel culture. Carissa wrote the '90s zine, *Screams From Inside*, which had both political essays and short stories.

J.M. Coetzee (1940–), winner of the Nobel Prize for Literature, was born in South Africa but left in the '60s. Despite his PhD, he was denied permanent residency in the US owing to his involvement in anti-Vietnam war activism. He is an outspoken animal rights activist, and in his 2007 post-modern book of essays disguised as a novel (or is it a novel disguised as a book of essays?) *Diary of a Bad Year*, he described his politics as anarchist:

> "If I were pressed to give my brand of political thought a label, I would call it pessimistic anarchistic quietism, or anarchist quietistic pessimism, or pessimistic quietist anarchism: anarchism because experience tells me that what is wrong with politics is power itself; quietism because I have my doubts about the will to set about changing the world, a will infected with the drive to power; and pessimism because I am skeptical that, in a fundamental way, things can be changed."

In the same book, he decries democracy:

> "[Democracy] does not allow for politics outside the democratic system. In this sense, democracy is totalitarian."

Alex Comfort (1920–2000), the author of the best-selling *The Joy of Sex*, said that he would much rather be remembered for his anarchism, his pacifism, and his novels (which include *On This Side of Nothing*). He also wrote an essay, *The Novel and Our Time*, exploring the novel as an agent of liberation.

Dennis Cooper (1953–), a sex-and-violence gay fiction writer, stirs up scandal with his rather darkly gory novels (such as *Try*). He comes from the 1970s punk scene and he edited and ran a zine for years before working for *Spin*. In an interview with *3 A.M. Magazine* in in 2001, he said, "I'm an anarchist, by philosophy. I believe everyone has everything they need within themselves to make the right decisions." WWW.DENNISCOOPER.NET

CrimethInc. (1995–) is an open group identity: anyone can compose a text or carry out an action and claim it for CrimethInc. In addition to organizing events, several CrimethInc. cells are known for producing books, magazines, records, and the like. Aside from allegedly non-fiction compositions such as *Days of War, Nights of Love*, the collective has published several works of fiction, including *The Secret World of Duvbo* and *The Secret World of Terijian*, as well as *Expect Resistance*, which mixes narrative and non-fiction throughout. WWW.CRIMETHINC.COM & WWW.CRIMETHINC.BE

Steve Cullen (n.d.) is the author of *The Last Capitalist: A Dream of a New Utopia* as well as a non-fiction book exploring the libertarian critique of education, both published by Freedom Press in the UK.

Rick Dakan (n.d.) is the author of the *Geek Mafia* series of books that follows a group of radical hacker con-artists as they trick right-wingers and corporations out of millions of dollars. WWW.RICKDAKAN.COM

J. Daniels (n.d.) released a parody of TinTin in the 1980s that featured TinTin as a radical anarchist unionist, entitled *The Adventures of TinTin: Breaking Free*.
TINTINREVOLUTION.FREE.FR

Dennis Danvers (1947–) is a professor and author who philosophically identifies with anarchism. Of particular note, he's written a strange novel *The Watch*, in which Peter Kropotkin comes back to life in 1999 as a young man in Richmond, Virginia, but his *The Fourth World* and his as-yet-unpublished young adult book *Cloverleaf* deal with anarchist themes and politics as well.
WWW.DENNISDANVERS.COM

Voltairine DeCleyre (1866–1912) was a poet and theorist who converted to anarchism in 1887 after the Haymarket trial shattered her faith in the American justice system. She was an early believer in "anarchism without adjectives," which meant that she didn't choose to identify specifically with communist, mutaualist, or individualist anarchism. She fought voraciously for the rights of women. The most famous piece of her fiction is "The Chain Gang," a short story included in *The Gates of Freedom*.

Joseph Déjacque (1821–1864), born in France, was the author who coined the term "libertarian" to distinguish anarchists from liberals (in a letter to Proudhon, whom he criticized for opposing feminism). Among other things, he wrote the fictional utopia *L'Humanisphère: Utopie anarchique*, which includes in its introduction the lines: "This book is not written in ink, and its pages are not sheets of paper ... it is a projectile, that I throw thousands of onto the streets of the civilized." The utopia was first serialized in *Le Libertaire*, the US's first anarcho-communist journal. Joseph was exiled from Napeleon's France for publishing radical poetry, and retreated for a number of years to the US before returning to France and dying in Paris.

Jim Dodge (1945–) is a bioregionalist theorist, an anarchist, and a writer. His novels explore a sort of modern folklore, often including magic amidst otherwise real-world events. In his bioregionalist essay "Living by Life", he says that anarchy is an intrinsic value to bioregionalism, and says: "Anarchy doesn't mean out of control, it means out of *their* control."

Kevin Doyle (1961–), a member of Ireland's anarchist Worker Solidarity Movement, has been a writer of fiction and non-fiction for years. His stories have appeared in a number of magazines, his interview with Noam Chomsky has appeared in *Chomsky On Anarchism*, and he has an unpublished novel, *Step F*. He's been involved in a number of campaigns over the years from pro-choice battles to No Borders campaigns. When I told him about this book project, he had some interesting things to say:

I think fiction is very important in our lives and in how we understand the world we find ourselves in. I think it is important to encourage and promote more writing from below. Some regard the writing process as "waffle" and a "waste of time"—maybe even "a diversion from the real struggle." I wouldn't agree at all. Writing from below is an essential part for me of creating an alternative culture and vital if we are to move anarchism into the broad center of world politics where it must be one day.

KFDOYLE.WORDPRESS.COM

Kristyn Dunnion (1969–), a vegan, queer anarchist from Canada, is the author of three novels for a wide age range of readers: *Missing Matthew, Mosh Pit,* and *Big Big Sky*. She's also a performance artist under the name Miss Kitty Galore, plays bass for dyke metal band Heavy Filth, and has helped organize the Toronto Anarchist Bookfair. WWW.KRISTYNDUNNION.COM

Isabelle Eberhardt (1877–1904), raised by a nihilist and anarchist, was a cross-dressing sufi and writer who traveled and wrote extensively throughout northern Africa before dying suddenly in a flash flood at the age of 27. She was accused of assisting indigenous resistance to French occupation, and generally had many strange adventures. She wrote short stories, journalism, and journal entries, most of which survive. Although she became more invested in sufism and Islam than in anarchism proper, I feel it is safe to consider her the anarchist she was raised to be.

J. G. Eccarius (1818–) is, according to his publishers, an anarchist vampire born in Germany and currently residing in Mexico and California who is a prolific writer of fiction. If his publishers, III Publishing, are to be believed, Eccarius was involved with both the First International and the IWW. His short stories have appeared in a number of magazines including *Fifth Estate,* and his novels include the curious *The Last Days of Jesus Christ the Vampire*.

Mattias Elftorp (1978–) is a comic book author from Malmö, Sweden. A politically involved anarchist and cyberpunk, he is the author of the *Piracy is Liberation* books, which he describes as "Political theory, filtered through autobiography, masked as fiction in the form of cyberpunk postapocalypse." Although most of his work is in English, he's done recurring "Arg Kanin" (Angry Animals) short comics in Swedish that are printed in different publications and are used on political fliers. He recently did an exhibition "Violence," on police brutality, that coincided with the European Social Forum being held in Malmö. WWW.ELFTORP.COM/FREEINFORMATION

Max Ernst (1891–1976) was an active participant in both Dada and Surrealism and was a visual artist who worked in collage, paintings, and sculpture. He was also one of the early creators of wordless novels, such as his *Une semaine de bonté* (A Week of Kindness), a collaged dark piece that follows a bird-man in a dark and surreal world. It wasn't hard to discover he was politically radical (as most dadaists and surrealists were), but it was from *Conversing with Cage*, a collection of interviews with anarchist composer John Cage edited by Richard Kostelanetz that I discovered Ernst as an anarchist. In one interview, Cage is talking about his own anarchist influences and mentions, "I said something about anarchy to the widow of Max Ernst and she said that Max was an anarchist."

Félix Fénéon (1861–1944) was an art and literary critic in turn-of-the-century Paris, the coiner of the term "neo-impressionism," and openly identified as an anarchist. In 1894, he and 29 others were acquitted of conspiracy to bomb and assassinate political leaders. He wrote *Novels in Three Lines*, a piece that redefined the idea of story-telling. The book is formed from a series of newspaper headlines that he wrote in 1906 for a paper, but taken together they paint a dark vignette of Parisian life.

Lawrence Ferlinghetti (1919–), the famous beat poet, has long identified as a philosophical anarchist and a pacifist—it was only two weeks after Nagasaki was bombed that he, as an American solider, visited the ruins. In the '50s he started the City Lights bookstore and publishing company in San Francisco, where he published Ginsberg's *Howl* and was therefore arrested and charged with obscenity. With the help of the ACLU, he won and set a legal landmark for other publishers of sex and drug literature. In addition to his poetry, he wrote two novels: *Her* (1960), a surreal and semi-autobiographical novel, and *Love in the Days of Rage* (1988), about a bourgeois anarchist caught up in the May '68 uprisings in Paris.

Leslie Fish (n.d.), an accomplished folk singer and one of the creators of the "Filk" tradition (science-fiction/fantasy themed music), is also an author, anarchist, and Wobbly. She once wrote a guide to surviving the apocalypse in the form of an album, *Firestorm*, in which she relayed information about making antibiotics, gunpowder, and lenses. She also practices that renown form of plagiarism, fan-fiction, having fan-published a novel taking place in the Star Trek universe. She took part in writing a collaborative fantasy trilogy, *The Sword of Knowledge*, of which she authored the first book, *A Dirge for Sabis*. www.LESLIEFISH.COM

Fly (n.d.), a comic author, has been squatting in New York City for over two decades. Her stories are beautifully honest and strange, fictionalizing elements of her life on the streets and in squats and traveling the world. Her work has been collected into the books *CHRON!IC!RIOTS!PA!SM!* and *Total Disaster*, as well as the graphic novel *Dog Dayz*. Her comic "Zero Content" appeared in *Slug & Lettuce* for years, and she's done the covers of countless books, zines, and records. www.FLYSPAGE.COM

William Godwin (1756–1836), considered by some "the first anarchist," did indeed lay down an impressive amount of anti-state theory, in part in his remarkably titled *Enquiry concerning Political Justice, and its Influence on General Virtue and Happiness*. He also, however, wrote what is considered the first mystery novel: *Things as They Are or The Adventures of Caleb Williams*. He was married to Mary Wollstonecraft, one of the first feminists, and fathered Mary Shelley, one of the first science-fiction authors. He was libeled and persecuted heavily for his political beliefs and spent much of his life living as anonymously as possible.

Paul Goodman (1911–1972), was a lot of things to a lot of different people. To the psychotherapy world, he is known as one of the co-founders of Gestalt theory. To the literary world, he was a novelist. Perhaps his most famous novel is *The Empire City*, a story that follows a '50s rebel in New York City. But he's also well known as the author of *Growing Up Absurd*, and his works were hugely influential on the '60s student radical movement, a movement he later criticized as sometimes both too dogmatic and too fickle.

Jimmy T. Hand (1984–) is an anarchist adventurer (to use his words) and writer. He's written two autobiographical novellas, *In the Hall of the Mountain King* and *The Road to Either Or*. He ran away from home, never finished high school, and never regretted either. He's been a part of anti-globalization, anti-war, and anti-logging activism, and has a tendency to travel.

M. John Harrison (1945–), author of the anarchist *The Centauri Device* among many other novels, said the following in an interview with Andy Darlington (*S.F. Spectrum* No.8, 1985):

> We must accept—given that [all viewpoints come down to subjectivity]—that we must operate personally. I mean, that's why I'm still an anarchist. If all value-judgements are subjective which they are by definition, linguistically and in the real world, then any evaluation we make of the universe is personal. It therefore behooves us to act with dignity, and act personally. Not to club together in big groups and say "because we have agreed on this personal evaluation as universal, from now on it will *be* universal, and we will hit anybody who doesn't agree with us!"

WWW.MJOHNHARRISON.COM

Jaroslav Hašek (1883–1923), a Czech whose satirical anti-war novel *The Good Soldier Švejk and His Fortunes in the World War* has been translated into more than 60 languages, was a notorious anarchist and political organizer in Prague. He spent a month in jail for assaulting an officer and he published an anarchist newspaper. In his later life, he shied away from his anarchist leanings and was a member of the Bolshevik Party. At one point, while employed by *The Animal Journal*, he was fired for writing about imaginary animals as though they were real.

Derrick Jensen (1960–) is a radical environmentalist and author and is considered one of the most influential anti-civilization thinkers. He is more famous for his non-fiction works such as *A Culture of Make-Believe* and *Endgame*, but he has also written a couple of novels, a graphic novel, and a book about teaching creative writing—a subject which he has taught in both prison and college. WWW.DERRICKJENSEN.ORG

Ba Jin (1904–2005) is considered one of the most important figures in Chinese literary history. He was introduced to anarchism at the age of 15 by Kropotkin's writing and he translated many anarchist works into Chinese for publication by a Shanghai newspaper. He worked on behalf of the struggle to free Sacco & Vanzetti and corresponded with Vanzetti until the Bostonian was executed. His most famous novel, *Family*, is a work critiquing the Chinese feudal system and promotes the concept of youth in revolt. In the 1950s, perhaps due to fear of persecution, he disavowed the anarchism of his youth, and even went to far as to purge his own works of their anarchistic content. Regardless, he was branded as a counter-revolutionary by the Cultural Revolution and was prevented from writing for years. When the Cultural Revolution passed, he rose in party favor and found himself Chairperson of the Chinese Writer's Association. In later writings, he alluded to possible resentment of his abandonment of anarchism.

James Kelman (1946–) is best known for his award-winning novel *How Late It Was, How Late It Was*, a stream-of-consciousness story about a shoplifter that the BBC refused to air readings of. His novels feature working class protagonists and he has written quite a bit about the nature of colonization. He spoke at the 2007 Bay Area Anarchist Bookfair and AK Press has published some of his work.

Margaret Killjoy (1982–) is the only one of these authors who got to write their own bio. Margaret performs as a songwriter and accordion player under the name Magpie Killjoy, founded *SteamPunk Magazine*, and has published fiction tales in *SteamPunk Magazine*, *Steamypunk*, and a few directly in zine form. WWW.BIRDS-BEFORETHESTORM.NET

Sergei "Stepniak" Kravchinski (1851–1895) was raised in Russia but left the Russian army to fight an insurgent war against the Turks in Bosnia. He then joined Errico Malatesta in 1877 for the first act of "propaganda by the deed:" a small uprising in Benevento, Italy. Some 30 armed anarchists marched on two towns and liberated the peasantry by burning the tax records. They were treated as heroes by the peasants, and were of course quickly arrested. Then Stepniak moved back to Russia and assassinated the chief of the secret police in the streets with a dagger and escaped. He moved to England and became a prolific novelist and playwright under the name "S. Stepniak." He was responsible, in a large part, for bringing the plight of the Russian peasantry under the Tzars to the attention of the English-speaking world. Indeed, he was the first Russian to write a novel in English. He was struck dead by a train while crossing the tracks one evening.

Gabriel Kuhn (1972–) is an Austrian-born anarchist writer currently living in Sweden. He spent ten years traveling five continents and was at one time a semi-professional soccer player (in fact, he's written the *Anarchist Football Manual*, an introduction to the radical politics of soccer). He publishes a large number of zines and pamphlets through Alpine Anarchist Productions, including a bunch of short stories. He also works with *Brand*—a swedish anarchist magazine that has been published continuously since 1898—as well as Unrast and PM Press.
WWW.ALPINEANARCHIST.ORG

Gustav Landauer (1870–1919) was a pacifist and an anarchist. His first book was a novel titled *Der todesprediger* (The Death Preacher). He spent his life in and out of jail for his politics, translated everything from Proudhon to Wilde, and explored the connections between mysticism and anarchism. He was stoned to death by the German army in 1919.

Bernard Lazare (1865–1903) was a Jewish French anarchist who was heavily in-fluential in French Zionist circles but disagreed wholeheartedly about the creation of a Jewish state. He traveled the whole of Europe, concerning himself with the plight of the Jewish proletariat. He also wrote extensively, and although he is better known for his essays about anti-semitism, he also wrote *La Porte d'ivoire* and *Les Porteurs de torches*, which are considered fiction (and which I can't find any English translation of, sadly!).

Ursula K. Le Guin (1929–) is perhaps the most renown living anarchist fiction writ-er. She was a pioneer of feminist science fiction, and her fantasy series *Earthsea* is read by a wide range of people of all ages. She is a pacifist and an anarchist, and al-though she has shied away from direct political organizing, she has certainly never shied from protests or political grunt-work. She spent 40 years translating Lao Tzu's *Tao Te Ching*, bringing out the radical thought in Taoist philosophy.
WWW.URSULAKLEGUIN.COM

John Henry Mackay (1864–1933) John Henry Mackay was an individualist anar-chist, homosexual, and author who wrote in German and was published in many places including the journal *Liberty*. *The Swimmer* is sometimes considered his finest novel, although he also wrote a series of books promoting and defending pederasty.

Riley MacLeod (1982–) is the author of *Against!*, an anarcho-queer retelling of the life of the Buddha. He was the co-founder and artistic director of sTaGes: the New York City Transgender Theatre Festival, and has worked extensively in NYC queer theater. He holds a Master's in Theology from Harvard Divinity School, as well as the dubious honor of being the school's first anarcho-queer trans punk.

Charles Malato (1857–1938) was the grandson of a Count—one who was ruthless in putting down insurrection—but Charles' father was a communard. Charles himself was often at odds with the law for his associations with anarchism and went into exile in London for a period. As a writer, he was primarily a journalist, but he also wrote the novel *La grande grève* (The Great Strike) about a 1901 miner's strike in France. *The New York Times* from June 5, 1905, when describing his arrest for conspiracy, remarks upon the "elaborate perfection of his manners," and that his articles were "remarkable for their polished grace."

Ethel Mannin (1900–1984) was a particularly prolific author who did much to draw attention to women's issues and anarchism in Britain. She wrote popular books: this is to say she wrote books for the populace, rather than for the educated minority. Of particular note is her *Red Rose*, a novel based on the life of Emma Goldman.

Dambudzo Marechera (1952–1987) was one of the most celebrated post-colonial African writers. Born into poverty in Rhodesia (later to become Zimbabwe) as one of nine children, he excelled in school. In fact, he showed such promise that he was accepted to and expelled from both the University of Rhodesia and, later, Oxford. (The former, he was kicked out for protesting racism. Oxford? Oxford he apparently tried to set fire to.) After being expelled from Oxford, he lived in squats in London. His first book, *The House of Hunger*, made him famous, but his nationalist post-colonial African peers criticized it and him for adopting a modernist, stream-of-consciousness style—at the time, it was thought that social realism and accessibility were important in drawing attention to Africa's plight. His response to this criticism? "If you are a writer for a specific nation or a specific race, then fuck you" (Interview and Discussion with Dambudzo Marechera about *Black Sunlight*," Veit-Wild, *Dambudzo Marechera*, 121). His next novel, *Black Sunlight*, was explicitly anarchist and mocked the nationalist, Marxist assumptions of most African libratory struggles. It was banned in Zimbabwe, where he eventually returned and spent the last few years of his life homeless before dying of AIDS.

Frans Masereel (1889–1972), a Flemish artist, a pacifist, an anarchist, and one of the most famous woodcut artists in history, consistently included his political values in his work. He pioneered the wordless novel, publishing such books as *Die Stadt* (The City), a 100-page story told only through pictures.

Paul Mavrides (1945–) is an underground comic book author and artist. He helped found *Anarchy Comics*, which ran for four issues between 1979 and 1987 and included comic-book renditions of anarchist history, theory, and fiction. He did illustration for the Union of Concerned Commies, a left-libertarian branch of the anti-nuke movement, including an iconic cop-car-on-fire shirt with the slogan "No Apologies." He was a founding member of The Church of SubGenius, and in the 1990s he fought the state of California when they tried to tax comic book writers as though they were commercial contractors instead of authors. It took years, but he won. In a 1997 interview with artie.com, he said, "If I have kept even one small child from growing up to become a Republican or Democrat my entire career will be justified. And, in the end—when all's said and done—isn't that what ART's all about?"

Ricardo Mella (1861–1925) was a Spanish anarchist, author of the anarchist novel *La nueva utopia* (The New Utopia). He published a number of political essays, and his theories were highly influential in the forming of the anarchist labor union the CNT. He also translated the works of Malatesta, Bakunin, and Kropotkin into Spanish.

Cody Meyocks (1989–) is an anarchist short story writer who works in a free-form style and self-publishes in print and online.

Louise Michel (1830–1905), the "Red Virgin of Montemartre," is one of the finest role models for any ethical school teacher, or really any radical at all. The daughter of a maid and a young gentleman, Louise became a school teacher but was fired repeatedly for her refusal to support Bonaparte III. She joined the Paris Commune and treated the wounded, pondered political assassination, and reportedly led the charge of 200 armed women against thousands of soldiers (and the soldiers, the story goes, refused orders to fire upon the women and drank wine with them instead). For all of this she was banished to New Caledonia, where she refused special treatment as a woman, taught the Kanak indigenous children, and joined the Kanak's uprising against their colonial rule. Then she returned to France and headed libertarian schools. The rest of her life was spent in and out of prison and traveling Europe in the promotion of anarchism. She also wrote a lot of fiction, non-fiction, and poetry, very little of which I can find in English. Her novels include *Le claquedents*, and the 953 page *La misère*.

Henry Miller (1891–1980) is famous for obscenity. That is, he's famous for his books *The Tropic of Cancer* and *The Tropic of Capricorn*, which were banned from publication in the US for nearly 30 years. His books are strange, rambling, and sexual, and they did a lot to revolutionize literature. He was briefly involved in the Socialist Party, but was far more influenced by the surrealists. In an interview in Frank L. Kersnowski and Alice Hughes' *Conversations with Henry Miller*, Henry says that an anarchist is "exactly what I am. Have been all my life. Without belonging, you know, without subscribing," considering himself a "little a" anarchist. Near the end of his life, he said: "[I am] even more [of an anarchist], today, though I lead what you would call a respectable life. The other day, just reading about Prince Kropotkin, who was my great favorite ... of course, 'anarchist', nobody here in America is an anarchist, you know. It's a meaningless term here. They confuse it with 'anarchy.'" [ibid.]

Octave Mirbeau (1848–1917) was a rather famous writer of the bizarre. In his younger life he was a patriot, but converted to anarchism in 1885. His novels included grotesque portraitures of modern society, including *The Torture Garden*, a book of depravity that is dedicated "To the priests, the soldiers, the judges, to those people who educate, instruct and govern men, I dedicate these pages of Murder and Blood." An early translation of his novel *The Diary of a Chambermaid* was refused publication in the US. His 1888 rant, *Voters Strike*, has the following wonderful quote: "Sheep run to the slaughterhouse, silent and hopeless, but at least sheep never vote for the butcher who kills them or the people who devour them. More beastly than any beast, more sheepish than any sheep, the voter names his own executioner and chooses his own devourer." Octave was also an outspoken supporter of Félix Fénéon and his comrades when they were arrested for conspiracy.

James Leslie Mitchell (1901–1935), a Scottish author who attained a certain amount of fame by writing about Scotland in *A Scots Quair* under the nom de plume Lewis Grassic Gibbon, was also an anti-civilization anarchist communist. He wrote a number of anti-civilization fantasy books, most famous of which is *Three Go Back*. He died young of peritonitis.

Federica Montseny (1905–1994), daughter of anarchist writer Joan Montseny, first published fiction in her family's periodicals at the age of 17. She continued to write, but during the revolutionary period of the Spanish Civil War she became Spain's first female minister of health, where she legalized abortion. Both her position in the government and her position on abortion were quite divisive in the anarchist movement. When the war was lost to the fascists, she and her family fled to France, where she stayed. She wrote primarily non-political fiction books, although she continued to travel and promote anarchism.

Joan Montseny, aka **Federico Urales** (1864–1942), a Catalan anarchist and secular schoolteacher (secular schools being a rare and radical thing at the time), was first arrested while protesting the death of the Haymarket martyrs. He was later exiled for his radicalism to the UK, but he returned to Spain under the name Federico Urales. Thereupon he began to publish writing, including a great deal of fiction in the journals he and his wife ran, *La Novela Ideal* and *La Novela Libre*. He was at times both an individualist and trade unionist, and was involved in the founding of both the CNT and the FAI (anarcho-syndicalist trade unions). When Franco's fascists won the Spanish Civil War, Federico and his wife and daughter fled to France, where he died.

Michael Moorcock (1939–) is one of the most prolific authors around, with over 100 novels to his name. He's an anarchist by philosophy, and he explores the concept of the anti-hero in nearly all of his books. Many historical characters, including the Ukrainian anarchist Nestor Makhno, make regular appearances in his stories. Although not as well-known today, his cultural influence runs deep and his work has spawned a great deal of imitations. He was an important part of the New Wave of science fiction writers who, in the late 1960s, transformed the genre by saving it from its clichés. WWW.MULTIVERSE.ORG

Alan Moore (1953–) is considered one of the most important writers in the field of comics, but he's also an anarchist and a practicing magician. Four of his books have been turned into major Hollywood movies (*V for Vendetta*, *Watchmen*, *From Hell*, and *The League of Extraordinary Gentlemen*), none with his permission.

Jim Munroe (n.d.) is a Canadian anarchist writer who works in many different mediums, from comics to novels to movies to videogames. He once, with a group of activist writers, wheat-pasted up one-page science fiction stories painting the horrors of gentrification in affected neighborhoods.

P.M. is the name that in the 1980s, an anonymous member of the Midnight Notes Collective wrote the book *Bolo'Bolo* under. It's considered one of the primary anarchist utopia novels. It discusses a decentralized, anti-authoritarian anarchist system. The same author has now released a second novel, *Akiba*.

Eugene Nelson (1929–1999), from Modesto, California, was a dedicated unionist farm worker, working with Caser Chavez. Later in life, he joined the IWW. He also wrote a great deal, include the history of the Wobblies and several novels, including *Bracero* and *Fantasia of a Revolutionary*.

Kenneth Patchen (1911–1972), pre-cursor to the Beats and perhaps the first jazz poet, was part of "The San Francisco Anarchist Circle" in the 1940s. He wrote a tirade against WWII and the US involvement in it (not a popular position) disguised as the novel *The Journal Of Albion Moonlight* (1941). With this move he guaranteed himself artistic obscurity for the rest of his career.

Antonio Penichet (?–1964) was an important Cuban anarcho-syndicalist who spent his life as a typesetter, organizer, and writer. His fiction was suppressed by the government, and he was jailed at one point, possibly sentenced to death in 1919 (if he was, I'm not sure how he got out of that). At the end of his life, he was a historian and librarian.

Fredy Perlman (1934–1984) is best known as the author of the beautiful and strange *Against His-tory, Against Leviathan*, an early anarcho-primitivist text. But he was also the author (under the character names of Yarostan Vochek and Sophie Nachalo) of *Letters of Insurgents*, a novel that takes the form of letters between two radicals many years after the heyday. Fredy, born in the city of Brno (in what is now the Czech Republic), immigrated to the US, got a doctorate and got arrested for protesting. He went to Paris and participated in the May '68 uprising. He and his life-partner Lorraine Perlman started Black & Red Publications. He helped translate the Situationists into English, and he helped publish *Fifth Estate* magazine. The Audio Anarchy project (WWW.AUDIOANARCHY.ORG) has a free audiobook of *Letters of Insurgents* available for download.

Henry Poulaille (1896–1980) was the son of an anarchist carpenter but was orphaned at 14. He grew up to become a publisher, editor, and novelist who fiercely advocated for proletarian literature. His novels were highly autobiographical fiction, and included his 1935 *Les damnés de la terre* (*The Wretched of the Earth*)—which is not to be confused with the significantly more famous *Les damnés de la terre* by Frantz Fanon that was published in 1961. Of course, the phrase is a reference to the first line of that famous leftist song "The Internationale," so this synchronicity is most likely a coincidence.

John Cowper Powys (1872–1963) wrote novels that are, by all accounts, long, winding, and complex. He corresponded with Emma Goldman for some time (their letters have now been published) and associated himself directly with anarchism, speaking with great hope and joy about the anarchists in the Spanish Civil War.

Eduard Pons Prades (1920–2007), historian and anti-fascist militant, was just 16 years old when he fought in the Spanish Civil War. He was wounded in the shelling of Barcelona, but went back to fighting once he recovered, in the Quinta del Biberón (the "Baby Bottle Brigade"). After Franco took Spain, he moved to France, where he helped the French Underground fight the Nazis. When Hitler was defeated, he went back to fighting Franco as a guerilla. Eventually, he settled a bit and became a historian and publisher. He wrote a novel as well, *La venganza* (*The Vengeance*).

Graham Purchase (n.d.) is the author of *My Journey With Aristotle to the Anarchist Utopia*, an intriguing novel that describes a bio-regionalist, green-syndicalist future. For better or worse, when I contacted III Publishing, his publisher, they told me he had left Australia and was living somewhere in India, without much communication to the outside world.

Sir Herbert Read (1893–1968) was an anarchist and a knight, which is pretty cool (or hypocritical, I suppose). Anyhow, he is best known for his poetry, but he wrote a novel as well, *The Green Child*, that explores totalitarianism in a fantastic setting. Here's a nice quote by him, from his *Poetry and Anarchism*:

> In order to create it is necessary to destroy; and the agent of destruction in society is the poet. I believe that the poet is necessarily an anarchist, and that he must oppose all organized conceptions of the State, not only those which we inherit from the past, but equally those which are imposed on people in the name of the future.

Gerry Reith (1959–1984) was an incessant zinester, correspondent, and anarchist writer who lived the last six years of his short life in Wyoming. He wrote large quantities of anarchist short fiction, some collected into the book he assembled *Neutron Gun*. After the local authorities intercepted his mail and reported him to the FBI, he took his own life. WWW.INSPIRACY.COM/MINITRUE

Cristy C. Road (1982–) is best known as a punk-rock illustrator who draws people of all shapes, sizes, and genders. She's done a fair amount of work with Food Not Bombs and other anarchist organizations, and she's been running zines for years, focusing on queer woman of color issues, and on punk. Her first novel, *Bad Habits*, came out in 2008, and while illustrated, owes more to Kathy Acker-style illustrated books than comics. WWW.CROADCORE.ORG

Donald Rooum (1928–) is the author and illustrator of the *Wildcat: Anarchist Cartoons* series, published by Freedom Press. Not to be mistaken for Wildcat, the DC Comics misogynist character. Also, not to be confused with the Wildcat detourned situationist comics (which are available online from the Bureau of Public Secrets).

Hugh Ryan (1978–) is a queer anarchist and writer. He writes essays and articles for magazines, websites, and literary journals, but he makes his living ghostwriting *The Hardy Boys*.

Hans Ryner (1861–1938) was an individualist pacifist anarchist, once heralded as "The Prince of Storytellers" by the readers of the radical press in France. But today his work (over 50 books of fiction, non-fiction, and poetry) is all but unavailable in

English. His activism was primarily around finding recognition for conscientious objector status in wartime, but he also rose to the defense of Sacco and Vanzetti. One of his novels, *Les pacifiques*, seems particularly interesting to me, and I'd love to read it: it is the tale of an anti-civilization, pacifist anarchist utopia on Atlantis.

Ilan Shalif (n.d.) is an Israeli psychologist and libertarian communist, who has authored numerous essays and books on self-help, including methods with which to quit smoking. He's active in Anarchists Against the Wall, a group of Israeli anarchists who use direct and symbolic action to challenge the apartheid wall between Israel and Palestine. He's also written a novella-length anarchist utopia, *Glimpses into the Year 2100*, about anarchist kibbutzim. WWW.SHALIF.COM

Robert Shea (1933–1994), co-author (with Robert Anton Wilson) of *The Illuminatus! Trilogy*, was also a publisher of an anarchist zine: *No Governor: A journal of anarchistic ideas, Ideas for Individuals.* Much of his work has been posthumously entered into the Creative Commons to be downloaded for free.

Lewis Shiner (1950–) is an author who writes what he feels like writing, refusing to stay in a single genre. He did, however, find himself one of the originators of cyberpunk, with his book *Frontera*. He also novelized Bob Black's famous essay "The Abolition of Work" into his book *Slam*. He founded the Fiction Liberation Front, through which he gives away nearly all of his work for free, and quite astoundingly, he has almost always refused to solve the major conflict in his books through violence. He's a card-carrying member of the IWW as well. WWW.LEWISSHINER.COM

Norman Spinrad (1940–) is a science fiction writer and syndicalist who has been publishing novels since the mid '60s. His 1969 novel *Bug Jack Barron* (a pre-cyberpunk tale) was serialized in the magazine *New Worlds* (when Michael Moorcock was editor) and, as a result of its alleged profanity, the magazine was banned from some distributors and its funding was questioned in the House of Commons. In an interview with *Locus Magazine* in February, 1999, he said:

> "All right, so I'm an anarchist—but I'm a syndicalist. You have to have organized anarchy, because otherwise it doesn't work.... Providing hope is something science fiction should be doing. It sounds arrogant to say it, but if we don't do it, who the hell will? One of the social functions of science fiction is to be visionary, and when science fiction isn't being visionary, it hurts the culture's visionary sense."

OURWORLD.COMPUSERVE.COM/HOMEPAGES/NORMANSPINRAD

Starhawk (1951–) is an activist involved in anti-war, anti-globalization, social justice, and environmentalist issues. She's a pagan anarchist and ecofeminist, and is a

prominent voice in the movement for solidarity between people who advocate different levels of tactics and different methods of organizing. She's also an excellent writer, and although she's more known for her non-fiction books, she's published two novels: *The Fifth Sacred Thing* and its prequel *Walking to Mercury*.
WWW.STARHAWK.ORG

Leo Tolstoy (1828–1910), the famous Russian author of *War and Peace*, is considered the founder of Christian Anarchism. He never identified with anarchism during his life, but only because he associated it with bomb-throwers. He said as much in his 1900 essay "On Anarchy:"

> The Anarchists are right in everything; in the negation of the existing order, and in the assertion that, without Authority, there could not be worse violence than that of Authority under existing conditions. They are mistaken only in thinking that Anarchy can be instituted by a revolution. But it will be instituted only by there being more and more people who do not require the protection of governmental power.... There can be only one permanent revolution—a moral one: the regeneration of the inner man.

B. Traven (n.d., possibly 1882–1969) is a bit of a mystery. There lived for a period of time a renowned yet anonymous author in Mexico, who wrote under the name "B. Traven." His works were immensely popular throughout Europe (and still are) while they went nearly unnoticed in the US, with the exception of *The Treasure of the Sierra Madre*, which was turned into a movie starring Humphery Bogart. His books were firmly anti-capitalist and pro-anarchist, and the current leading theory as to his identity is that he was a German anarchist who went by the name of Red Marut. Marut published a German-language anarchist paper for several years, and joined in the ill-fated Bavarian Soviet in 1919 (which, based in Munich, fought against the Bolsheviks but was crushed eventually by the Germans). Traven's fiction first came to fame after his novel *The Ship of Death* was banned by Hitler.

Adrián del Valle (1872–1945) was an anarchist, journalist, and fiction writer who was greatly influential in Cuban anarchism. Born in Catalonia but moving to Havana in 1895 after time in NYC, Adrián wrote extensively for anarchist newspapers and had at least 15 fiction pieces published in Joan Montseny's *Novels de Libre* anarchist fiction journal. He was well received in both mainstream and radical literature worlds, and he also ran an anarchist health magazine *Pro-Vida*.

Jules Vallès (1832–1885) was a French journalist who ran a socialist/anarchist newspaper during the French commune (as well as fighting on the barricades, of course!) and escaped later repercussions by fleeing to England, where he wrote

several semi-autobiographical novels while continuing his career as a radical journalist. Most famous and still-in-print (owing to its less-political nature) of these
novels is *The Child*.

Kurt Vonnegut (1922–2007), famous satirist and author of *Slaughterhouse Five*
among many other books, was an ardent pacifist, anarchist, and world citizen. In
fact, he said as much in response to verbal attacks made against him in regards
to a speech of his at the Library of Congress: "The beliefs I have to defend are so
soft and complicated, actually, and, when vivisected, turn into bowls of undiffer-
entiated mush. I am a pacifist, I am an anarchist, I am a planetary citizen, and so
on" (Obituary from GUARDIAN.CO.UK). His final work was a book of political non-
fiction, *A Man Without a Country*.

Lois Waisbrooker (1826–1909), an early anarcha-feminist, wrote numerous essays
and novels (including *A Sex Revolution*), edited the anarchist newspaper *Lucifer*,
and was condemned in the early twentieth century for obscenity for re-printing the
word "penis" from official USDA documents. She lived at least part of her life at
"Home," an anarchist community in Washington State.

Oscar Wilde (1854–1900) was an important writer and socialite in Victorian London. The extent of Oscar Wilde's radicalism has, like so many famous people's,
been fairly well buried since his death. He promoted socialism only as a method
that he felt would lead to individualism, and, after reading the works of Kropotkin,
declared his anarchism: "I think I am rather more than a Socialist. I am something
of an Anarchist, I believe, but, of course, the dynamite policy is very absurd indeed" (From an interview in *Theatre*, 1894). He also published work in the anarchist magazine *Liberty*. Another Wilde quote of note (from his *The Soul Of Man
Under Socialism*):

> People sometimes inquire what form of government is most suitable for
> an artist to live under. To this question there is only one answer. The form
> of government that is most suitable to the artist is no government at all.

appendix B:
ALSO OF NOTE

These are some of many authors who, while not anarchists themselves (or having been anarchists only for select periods of their lives), seem important enough to mention.

Hugo Ball (1886–1927) was a founder of Dada, the anti-art movement. Inspired by Bakunin and anarchism in general, Dada was an attempt to destroy the contemporary art world. In Germany, at least, it was also an inherently political movement, opposed to militarism and the state in general. Hugo Ball is best known for his nonsensical poetry, but he also wrote the only Dada novel, *Tenderenda the Fantast*. After breaking with Dada, he became a sort of Catholic pacifist, and remained obsessed with anarchism for the rest of his life, although he was turned off enough by the militancy that he avoided labeling himself with the term. My favorite quote by him is from *Flight Out Of Time*:

> The war is based on a crass error. Men have been mistaken for machines. Machines, not men, should be decimated. At some future date when only the machines march, things will be better. Then everyone will be right to rejoice when they all demolish each other.

William S. Burroughs (1917–1997), famous for *Naked Lunch* and other "cut-up" style books, wrote *Cities of the Red Night*, a remarkably homo-erotic book about the founding of left-libertarian societies modeled after the famed (and possibly fictional) pirate Captain Mission.

Albert Camus (1913–1960) never identified as an anarchist, but the anarchist movement could not have had a better friend in the author. He wrote for several anarchist newspapers regularly throughout his life, and he often used his fame and clout to get anarchist militants released. His non-fiction book *The Rebel* laid out exactly what was wrong with authoritarian socialism, and he was a staunch opponent of Stalinism.

Joseph Conrad (1857–1924) was born to Apollo Korzeniowski, a polish political radical and playwright who had ties to Bakunin. After participating in a revolt against the Russians, his father was taken to a camp in Russia where he died. Joseph, however, went on to make gross misrepresentations of anarchists in his books, jumping on the "bearded men with bombs hellbent on destruction" band-wagon of that time, with the novel *The Secret Agent* and the story *An Anarchist*. Ironically, *The Secret Agent* is considered to have been an inspirational text for Ted Kaczynski (The "Unabomber").

Philip K. Dick (1928–1982), American cult author, wrote one of his first novelettes explicitly on anarchism: *The Last of the Masters*. Although he did not side entirely with the anarchists, he stayed a proponent of governmental decentralization and was opposed to organized religion. His work is also immensely influential on anarcho-gnostics.

James Joyce (1882–1941) is the author of *A Portrait of an Artist as a Young Man* and perhaps the most famous Irish writer in history. It is contested that Joyce was actively an anarchist in his younger years (interested in both syndicalism and individualism) and a "philosophical anarchist" to a greater and lesser extent throughout the rest of his life.

Alan Grant (1949–), comic writer known for his *Batman* and *Judge Dredd* comics to the regular world and for the anarchist "super-villian" *Anarky* to us anarchists, was for time in the 1990s considering himself an anarchist. He has later gone on to embrace a "Neo-Tech" philosophy and no longer considers himself an anarchist, although he appears to remain sympathetic to anarchism and the early incarnations of *Anarky* are quite wonderful.

Robert Heinlein (1907–1988), considered by many anarchists to be hopelessly capitalistic and misogynistic, wrote a book *The Moon is a Harsh Mistress* that is still popular among anarchists, featuring as it does a sympathetic "wise old man" character who presents the concept of the "rational anarchist" and makes several valid arguments for anarchism. Before he began to write fiction, and before he began to explore right-wing politics (he supported the Vietnam War, among other things), Heinlein also was heavily involved in leftist author Upton Sinclair's bid for governor of California.

Frank Herbert (1920–1986) wrote the *Dune* novels, which are considered some of the finest speculative fiction ever written and are some of the first "ecological science fiction" books. Although he wasn't known to identify specifically with anarchism (and seemed eschew nearly all labels and easily-identifiable ideologies), he was immensely and constantly critical of government. He lived on a sustainable land project, complete with passive solar systems and the like, and he developed the idea of technopeasantry, a precursor to post-civilized theory and the appropriate technology movements. My favorite quote by him is from *Chapterhouse: Dune*:

Give me the judgment of balanced minds in preference to laws every time. Codes and manuals create patterned behavior. All patterned behavior tends to go unquestioned, gathering destructive momentum.

Also, from *Children of Dune*:

Governments, if they endure, always tend increasingly toward aristocratic forms. No government in history has been known to evade this pattern. And as the aristocracy develops, government tends more and more to act exclusively in the interests of the ruling class—whether that class be hereditary royalty, oligarchs of financial empires, or entrenched bureaucracy.

Aldous Huxley (1894–1963), author of the famous dystopian *Brave New World* and the less-renown utopian *Island*, eventually found his beliefs shifting towards anarchism. To quote Brian Crabtree's *The History of Anarchism*, "in the 'Foreword' of the 1946 edition [of *Brave New World*], he said that he believed that only through radical decentralization and a politics that was 'Kropotkinesque and cooperative' could the dangers of modern society be escaped."

Franz Kafka (1883–1924), author of *The Trial*, is remembered by the word "Kafkaesque," used to describe the convolutions of bureaucracy. What is less remembered is his near-silent participation in Czech anarchist meetings and occasional demonstrations for years, his extensive reading of and homages to anarchist theoriticians and writers, his involvement in the starting of an anarchist journal in Prague.

Jack London (1876–1916), famous for having written *The Call of the Wild*, was an active socialist and noted plagiarist. He was occasionally sympathetic to anarchists, although in an unpublished introduction to Alexander Berkman's *Prison Memoirs of an Anarchist*, London espoused that anarchist methods were inferior to those he promoted.

William Morris (1834–1896) was the man who attempted to reconcile the anarchists and the Marxists in Britain's Socialist League (he often sided with the anti-statists, although he never identified as more than a "semi-anarchist"). He failed at that task, but he did write the highly influential utopia *News From Nowhere* as well as develop the concept of fictional worlds to be utilized in fantasy fiction. Professionally, he designed wallpapers and typesets. A book-lover's radical, to be sure.

Nadar (1820–1910) was a celebrity-hound socialite of France. He was famous then for his novels, and is famous now as a groundbreaking photographer: he took the first aerial photos, he took the first underground photos, he took the first photos by artificial light. He also took most of the pictures of Proudhon, Bakunin, and

Kropotkin that we often see today. He corresponded with anarchist Élisée Reclus and he helped form a balloon battalion for the protection of the Paris Commune. It's unconfirmed whether he identified as an anarchist himself.

George Orwell (1903–1950), British novelist and critic of totalitarianism, never considered himself an anarchist, although, particularly in his early adulthood, he was to be found in anarchist circles. He also fought in the Spanish Civil War, and claims that, had he been more informed, he would have fought in the anarchist army instead of the Marxist. From his *The Road to Wigan Pier*: "I worked out an anarchistic theory that all government is evil, that the punishment always does more harm than the crime and the people can be trusted to behave decently if you will only let them alone," but also, "It is always necessary to protect peaceful people from violence. In any state of society where crime can be profitable you have got to have a harsh criminal law and administer it ruthlessly."

Victor Serge (1890–1947) began his political life as an anarchist (as an individualist), working for anarchist papers and getting involved in the Bonnot Gang, but eventually joined the Bolsheviks during their revolution. As a redeeming factor, he held that, in the arts, freedom of expression should hold true (a minority opinion among state communists). He was quite critical of Stalin and was exiled. He wrote, among other things, a good number of novels, including the anti-Stalin book *The Case of Comrade Tulayev*, and *Birth of Our Power*, about the anarchists in Barcelona. Much of his writing was done while in jail or on the run, and many of his manuscripts were destroyed by Stalinist police.

George Bernard Shaw (1856–1950) is remembered for his plays but he also wrote at least four novels, including *An Unsocial Socialist*. He is known to have flirted with both anarchism and Marxism before moving on to the social-democratic Fabian Society, where he remained a contentious, libertarian sort. He included sympathetic anarchists in his plays and was published by anarchist papers. One quote of his in particular (from a 1933 speech in New York) stands out:

> The ordinary man is an anarchist. He wants to do as he likes. He may want his neighbour to be governed, but he himself doesn't want to be governed. He is mortally afraid of government officials and policemen.

Mary Shelley (1797–1851), the author of *Frankenstein* (and therefore a founder of science-fiction), was the daughter of William Godwin, a founder of modern anarchism, and Mary Wollstonecraft, a founder of modern feminism. She was an outspoken vegetarian and was often a fan of her father's philosophical work.

Upton Sinclair (1878–1968), a socialist journalist and novelist, is best known for his first success, *The Jungle*, but he also wrote a book, *Boston*, in which he declared the innocence of anarchists Sacco and Vanzetti. What's interesting to learn now is that, through his correspondence, it has come to light that Sinclair may have actually believed that one or the other of the two anarchists was guilty, but that he felt it important, for various reasons, to continue to declare their innocence.

J.R.R. Tolkien (1892–1973), author of *The Lord of the Rings* (which has been critiqued as a vindication of the British middle class by a range of radical authors from Michael Moorcock to China Miéville) wrote the following to his son in 1943 (from *The Letters of J. R. R. Tolkien*):

> My political opinions lean more and more to Anarchy (philosophically understood, meaning abolition of control not whiskered men with bombs)—or to 'unconstitutional' Monarchy. I would arrest anybody who uses the word State (in any sense other than the inanimate realm of England and its inhabitants, a thing that has neither power, rights nor mind); and after a chance of recantation, execute them if they remain obstinate!... Government is an abstract noun meaning the art and process of governing and it should be an offence to write it with a capital G or so as to refer to people.... The most improper job of any man, even saints, is bossing other men. Not one in a million is fit for it, and least of all those who seek the opportunity.

Jules Verne (1828–1905) gave us the anti-hero Captain Nemo in *20,000 Leagues Under the Sea*, but he also wrote *The Survivors of the Jonathon*, featuring a sympathetic anarchist protagonist. It is likely that Kaw-Djer, this anarchist, was based on Verne's real life anarchist friend Élisée Reclus. Verne clearly had sympathies towards anarchism, but he spent much of his life as an elected official and took nothing resembling radical action after passing out pamphlets as a young man in the 1848 French Revolution.

Robert Anton Wilson (1937–2007), best known as the co-author (along with Robert Shea) of the discordian anarchist-conspiracy-theorist *Illuminatus Trilogy*, was once an anarchist but, by the end of his life, was not (from an interview by Jeffrey Elliot):

> My early work is politically anarchist fiction, in that I was an anarchist for a long period of time. I'm not an anarchist any longer, because I've concluded that anarchism is an impractical ideal. Nowadays, I regard myself as a libertarian. I suppose an anarchist would say, paraphrasing what Marx said about agnostics being "frightened atheists," that libertarians are simply frightened anarchists. Having just stated the case for the opposition, I will go along and agree with them: yes, I am frightened. I'm a libertarian because I don't trust the people as much as anarchists do. I want to see government limited as much as possible; I would like to see

it reduced back to where it was in Jefferson's time, or even smaller. But I would not like to see it abolished. I think the average American, if left totally free, would act exactly like Idi Amin. I don't trust the people any more than I trust the government.

appendix C: LISTS

For the past few years, I've been studying anarchist representation in fiction. These lists are compiled as part of that research. Note that I haven't personally read even half the books on these lists, but I spent a good bit of time researching every one. I'm certain this list isn't complete. These are just what I've found thus far.

I've found that books which represent anarchism have tended to fall into one of four categories. There are books, usually speculative fiction, which describe anarchist societies. Then there are those which contain sympathetic anarchist characters: these books can be all across the board from a sympathetic arsonist who mentions Bakunin to books with anarchist protagonists who avoid such simplifying stereotypes. Then there are historical fiction books that address important moments in our history. And finally, there is the old anarchist-as-bogeyman, nihilist-with-bomb villain that's so common in mainstream culture. But even among these books, there are doubtless many that anarchists would find useful, such as Zola's Germinal. *One sad thing I've noticed is there seems to be a resurgence of the anarchist-as-mindless-or-misguided saboteur stereotype in the past few years, one that I think can possibly be blamed on the recent resurgence of neo-Victorian fiction.*

Stories that explore anarchist societies:
Poul Anderson: *The Last of the Deliverers* (1957)
Anonymous, probably Hakim Bey: *Visit Port Watson!* (1985)
C.R. Ashbee: *The Building of Thelema* (1910)
Iain Banks: *The Culture* series (1987-2008)
John Barnes: *The Man Who Pulled Down the Sky* (1987)
John M. Batchelor: *A Strange People* (1888) (rumored)
Charles Willing Beale: *The Ghost of Guir House* (1895)
Walter Besant & James Rice: *The Monks of Thelema* (1880)
Gene Brewer: *K-PAX* series (1995-2007)
Dorothy Bryant: *The Kin of Ata Are Waiting for You* (1971)
Anonymous aka Beatrice May Butt aka W. H. Alhusen: *The Laws of Leflo* (1911)
Chris Carlsson: *After the Deluge* (2004)
Steve Cullen: *The Last Capitalist: A Dream of a New Utopia* (2002)
Samuel Delany: *Trouble on Triton* (1976)
Joseph Déjacque: *L'Humanisphère, Utopie anarchique* (1858)
L. Timmel Duchamp: Five books of the *Marq'ssan Cycle* (2005-2008)
Jane Doe: *Anarchist Farm* (1996)
Philip K. Dick: *The Last of the Masters* (1954)

Greg Egan: *Distress* (1995)
George Foy: *The Memory of Fire* (2000)
Homer Eon Flint: *The Queen of Life* (1919) (the author is thought to have died while robbing a bank)
Gabriel de Foigny: *A New Discovery of Terra Incognita Australis; or, The Southern World* (1676)
Bert Garskof: *The Canbe Collective Builds a Be-Hive* (1977)
Lewis Grassic Gibbon: *Three Go Back* (1932)
M. Gilliland: *The Free* (1990)
Rex Gordon: *Utopia 239* (1955)
Martin H. Greenberg & Mark Tier [editors]: *Freedom!* (an anthology, 2006)
George Griffith: *The Angel of the Revolution: A Tale of the Coming Terror* (1894)
Harry Harrison: *The Stainless Steel Rat Gets Drafted* (1987)
James P. Hogan: *Voyage from Yesteryear* (1999)
Cecelia Holland: *Floating Worlds* (1975)
Captain Charles Johnson, probably actually Daniel Defoe: *A General History of the Pyrates* (1724) (Look for "Captain Mission")
Ursula K. Le Guin: *The Dispossessed* (1974)
Saab Lofton: *A.D.* (1995)
Ken MacLeod: *Fall Revolution* series (1995–1999)
Ricardo Mella: *La nueva utopia* (somewhere between 1885–1889?)
Pat Murphy: *The City, Not Long After* (1989)
Alice Nunn: *Illicit Passage* (1993)
Emile Pataud & Emile Pouget: *How We Shall Bring About the Revolution* (1909)
Marge Piercy: *Woman on the Edge of Time* (1976)
P.M.: *Bolo'Bolo* (1985)
François Rabelais: *The Very Horrific Life of Great Gargantua, Father of Pantagruel* (1500s)
Adam Roberts: *Salt* (2000), *Gradisil* (2006)
John Scalzi (editor): *METAtropolis* (2009)
Norman Spinrad: *Child of Fortune* (1985)
Kim Stanley Robinson: *Mars* Trilogy (1992–1996)
Rudy Rucker: *Software* (1997)
Joanna Russ: *The Female Man* (1975)
Eric Frank Russell: *Late Night Final* (1948), *And Then There Were None* (1951), *The Great Explosion* (1962)
Han Ryner: *Les pacifiques* (1914)
José Saramago: *Seeing* (2004)
Robert Sheckley: *Skulking Permit* (1954)
Joan Slonczewski: *A Door into Ocean* (2000)
Charles Stross: *Singularity Sky* (2003)
Jonathan Swift: *Gulliver's Travels* (1726)

Andres Vaccari: *A Song for Sumerica* (unpublished)

A. E. van Vogt: *null-A* series (1948–1985), *The Anarchistic Colossus* (1977)

Elizabeth Waterhouse: *The Island of Anarchy: A Fragment of History in the 20th Century* (1887)

H.G. Wells: *Men Like Gods* (1923)

Stanley G. Weinbaum: *Valley of Dreams* (1934)

Stories that fictionalize anarchist history:

Horst Bienek: *Bakunin: An Invention* (1977) (about Bakunin)

Alan Burns: *The Angry Brigade* (1973) (about Britian in the 1970s)

Pino Cacucci: *Without A Glimmer of Remorse* (1994) (about the Bonnot gang)

Douglas Day: *The Prison Notebooks of Ricardo Flores Magon* (1991) (about the Mexican Revolution)

Martin Duberman: *Haymarket* (2005) (about the Haymarket Affair)

Frank Harris: *The Bomb* (1908) (about the Haymarket Affair)

Emanuel Litvinoff: *A Death out of Season* (1973) (about the Whitechapel siege of 1911)

Pedro de Paz: *The Man Who Killed Durrutti* (2005) (about what the title suggests)

Ramón J. Sender: *Seven Red Sundays* (1936) (about Madrid 1930s)

Victor Serge: *Birth of Our Power* (1931) (about a CNT uprising in Barcelona)

Wallace Stegner: *Joe Hill* (1950) (about the IWW, considered slander by many)

Paco Ignacio Taibo II: *Just Passing Through* (2000) (about Sebastian San Vincente, an anarchist labor organizer in Mexico in the 1920s)

Seth Tobocman: *War in the Neighborhood* (2000) (NYC squatters in the late '80s, early '90s)

Kent Winslow: *Dream World* (1990) (fictionalized autobiography)

Stories that feature sympathetic anarchist characters:

Jake Arnott: *Johnny Come Home* (2006)

Don Bannister: *Hard Walls of Ego* (1987)

Barrington J. Bayley: *Annihilation Factor* (1972) (somewhere between sympathetic and slander)

Louky Bersianik: *The Euguelionne* (1976)

Luciano Bianciardi: *La vita agra* (It's a Hard Life) (1962)

Charles Bock: *Beautiful Children* (2008)

Ben Burgis: *Three Perspectives on the Role of Anarchists in the Zombie Apocalypse* (2008)

Melvin Burgess: *Junk* (1996) (released as *Smack* in the US)

Daniel A. Coleman: *The Anarchist: A Novel* (2001)

Rick Dakan: *Geek Mafia: Black Hat Blues* (2009)

Dennis Danvers: *The Watch: A Novel* (2002)

Cory Doctorow: *Someone Comes to Town, Someone Leaves Town* (2005)

E. L. Doctorow: *Ragtime* (1975)

Louise M. Gagneur: *The Nihilist Princess* (1881)
William Gibson & Bruce Sterling: *The Difference Engine* (1990)
M. John Harrison: *The Centauri Device* (1974)
Gwyneth Jones: *I Am an Anarchist* (2002)
Maurice Leblanc: 21 *Arsène Lupin* novels (1907–1939)
Léo Malet: *Fog on the Tolbiac Bridge* (1956)
Eduardo Mendoza: *The City of Marvels* (1986)
Pat Mills: 10 *Nemesis the Warlock* books (1980–1999) (Most of Pat Mills' comics
     feature class war and anti-authoritarianism)
Wu Ming: *54* (2002)
Henry de Montherlant: *Chaos & Night* (1963)
Grant Morrison: *The Invisibles* (1994–2000)
Walter Mosley: *Archibald Lawless, Anarchist at Large* (2005)
E. Nesbit: *The Prophet's Mantle* (1885)
John Dos Passos: *U.S.A.* Trilogy (1930–1936)
Fernando Pessoa: *The Anarchist Banker* (1922)
Emeric Pressburger: *Killing a Mouse on Sunday* (1961)
Thomas Pynchon: *Against the Day* (2006)
Mack Reynolds: *Commune 2000 A.D.* (1974)
Spain Rodriguez: *Trashman* comics (1968-1985)
John Sayles: *The Anarchists' Convention* (1979)
Robert Sheckley: *The Resurrection Machine* (1989), *Simul City* (1990)
Brian Francis Slattery: *Liberation: Being the Adventures of the Slick Six After the
     Collapse of the United States of America* (2008)
Colin Spencer: *Anarchists in Love* (1963)
Norman Spinrad: *Little Heroes* (1987), *Greenhouse Summer* (2000)
Bruce Sterling: *Bicycle Repairmen* (published in *A Good Old-Fashioned Future*,
     1999)
Colm Tóibín: *The South* (1990)
T.H. White: *The Book of Merlyn* (written 1941, published 1977)
Richard Whiteing: *No. 5 John Street* (1899)

Stories that Feature Anarchists as Villains:
Isaac Babel: *Old Man Makhno* (1926?)
John Blazewick: *In the Shadow of Chaos* (2005)
A. Bertram Chandler: *The Anarch Lords* (1981)
G. K. Chesterton: *The Man Who was Thursday* (1908)
Joseph Conrad: *The Secret Agent* (1907), *An Anarchist* (1905), *Under Western
     Eyes* (1911)
Fyodor Dostoevsky: *The Devils* (also translated as *The Possessed* or *Demons*) (1872)
E. Douglas Fawcett: *Hartmann The Anarchist: or The Doom of the Great City* (1893)
Anatole France: *Penguin Island* (1908) (Arguably sympathetic. Note that France

did defend anarchist artist Aristide Delannoy when the latter was imprisoned for lampooning imperialists.)

Kerry Greenwood: *Death at Victoria Dock* (2006)

Henry James: *The Princess Casamassima* (1908)

Laurie R. King: *Touchstone* (2007)

Dean Koontz: *The Face* (2004)

Andrew Kreisberg: *Helen Killer* #1–4 (2008) (In which Helen Keller is given the power to see so she can fight anarchists. In real history, Helen Keller was a committed socialist, not a patriot.)

Dennis Lehane: *The Given Day* (2008)

Larry Niven: *Cloak of Anarchy* (1972)

Jana G. Oliver: *Virtual Evil* (2007), *Madman's Dance* (2008)

Robin Paige: *Death in Hyde Park* (2005)

Anne Perry: *The Whitechapel Conspiracy* (2001) and *Long Spoon Lane* (2005)

Neil Palmer: *Vegan Reich* (1998)

Helen & Olivia Rossetti as "Isabel Meredith": *A Girl Among the Anarchists* (1903)

April Smith: *Judas Horse* (2008)

Jo Soares: *Twelve Fingers: Biography of an Anarchist: A Novel* (2001)

Robert Louis Stevenson & Fanny Van de Grift Stevenson: *The Dynamiter* (1885)

Donald Thomas: *Sherlock Holmes and the King's Evil* (2009) [In which Holmes helps Churchill fight real-life anarchist Peter the Painter. Other Holmes stories that feature anarchist antagonists include "Danny Jones and the Great Detective" (1978) by an anonymous author, "Sherlock Holmes and the Boulevard Assassin" (1999) by John Hall, "The Case of the Disappearing Despatch Case" (1983) by Brian Ball, "The Adventure of the Bulgarian Diplomat" (1997) by Zakaria Erzinçlioglu, "The Affair of the Counterfeit Countess" (1998) by Craig Shaw Gardner, "The Pandora Plague" (1981) by Lee A. Matthias, and "The Diamond Jubilee" (year unknown) by Alan Downing.]

Eleanor Updale: *Montmorency and the Assassins* (2005), *Montmorency's Revenge* (2006)

H.G. Wells: *The Stolen Bacillus* (1893)

Donald E. Westlake as Curt Clark: *Anarchaos* (1967)

Carlos Ruiz Zafón: *The Shadow of the Wind* (2001)

Émile Zola: *Germinal* (1885) (Note that Zola *did* defend anarchist poet Laurent Tailhade in court, defending the right to write articles declaring the need to kill the Czar.)

Acknowledgements

First and foremost, I would like to thank **the authors** for sharing their time and their knowledge. And **Kim Stanley Robinson**, for writing the introduction and offering his hand in solidarity with anarchism. But certainly, this book was only possible thanks to the help of many others: **Kate Khatib**, my editor, for helping in every step of the process. **My father**, for turning me into a science-fiction fan. **Ratchet**, for hitching two days with me to conduct an interview. **Ben Beck**, for compiling the finest list of anarchist science fiction available. **Stewart Home**, for his essay on the fictional representation of anarchists. **AK Press**, for publishing the damn thing. **Zwarte Sanne, John Duda, Flint, Rhyd Wildermouth, Jesse Cohn, Reginazabo, Esther Eberhardt, Kurt Amacker, Crispin Sartwell, David Westling, Gabriel Kuhn, Kristyn Dunnion,** and **Gwilym** for their invaluble research assistance. Asheville's **Black Cover Book Club** for letting me make them discuss books by my interviewees. **Infoshop.org**, for publishing some of these interviews as I went. **Colin Foran**, for his beautiful cover illustration. **Libby Bulloff** and **Charles Eberhardt** for their design advice. And I want to thank **the radical scenes of Asheville and Baltimore as a whole**, because as much as I sometimes pretend otherwise, I don't exist in a vacuum and I love my friends.

Support AK Press

AK Press is one of the world's largest and most productive anarchist publishing houses. We're entirely worker-run and democratically managed. We operate without a corporate structure—no boss, no managers, no bullshit. We publish close to twenty books every year, and distribute thousands of other titles published by other like-minded independent presses from around the globe.

The Friends of AK program is a way that you can directly contribute to the continued existence of AK Press, and ensure that we're able to keep publishing great books just like this one! Friends pay a minimum of $25 per month, for a minimum three month period, into our publishing account. In return, Friends automatically receive (for the duration of their membership), as they appear, one **free** copy of **every** new AK Press title. They're also entitled to a 20% discount on **everything** featured in the AK Press Distribution catalog and on the website, on **any** and **every** order. You or your organization can even sponsor an entire book if you like!

Won't you be our friend? Email friendsofak@akpress.org for more info, or visit http://www.akpress.org/programs/friendsofak